The Kingdom of God and North-East England

Opposite, clockwise from top right:

Minsteracres Community Resource Centre, Minsteracres, Shepherd's Law, Sheraton Grange Comprehensive School, Minsteracres.

The Kingdom of God and North-East England

Edited by JAMES D. G. DUNN
with J. I. McDONALD,
PETER SEDGWICK
and ALAN M. SUGGATE

SCM PRESS LTD

British Library Cataloguing in Publication Data

The Kingdom of God and North-east England.
  1. Sociology, Christian
  I. Dunn, James D. G.
  261.1   BT738

  ISBN 0–334–00837–9

First published 1986
by SCM Press Ltd
26–30 Tottenham Road, London N1

Phototypeset by Input Typesetting Ltd, London
and printed in Great Britain by
Richard Clay (The Chaucer Press) plc
Bungay, Suffolk.

Contents

Preface

In January 1985 a number of scholars (mainly biblical) met at Fircroft College, Birmingham, at the invitation of the Foundation for the Study of Christianity and Society. The conference had been called to examine the question of biblical authority and its role in relation to the various important moral and social issues which confront us today. In particular, if the Bible still provides a source and resource, a guide and norm for our corporate faith and its outworkings, how should we expect it to function in these roles today? Does the Bible allow us to talk of a Christian vision (or visions) of society? Can we speak meaningfully of 'the biblical solution' to particular moral and ethical problems?

Throughout the discussion there was a general concern that the work of biblical scholarship should not be seen merely as a historical description which at best provides useful pegs for the real work of the systematic or moral theologian, the biblical expositions which could be safely confined to the opening section of a report and then be as good as forgotten for all the difference they made. For the Bible to function properly as resource or norm (canon) meant that there needed to be greater integration of the specialist skills and contributions of the biblical scholar with those of other members of the Christian community in wrestling with the problems of today. To interpret life with the help of the Bible requires a greater cooperative effort among scholars, policy formers and people 'at the coal face' than has been the case hitherto.

What follows describes one of the projects which sprang from that conference. The challenge was obvious. A concern to be 'biblical' found a ready test-case in Jesus' proclamation of the kingdom of God. And for those of us who live and work in the North East of England a concern for the social problems and realities of today need look no further than our own doorstep.

The challenge was to test whether the two could be brought together in any meaningful and helpful way.

The group who met initially consisted of Bruce Chilton, from the Department of Biblical Studies, Sheffield, who has both written and edited books on the kingdom, Peter Sedgwick the Theological Consultant to the North East churches, and Alan Suggate (Social Ethics) and myself (New Testament), both from the Department of Theology in Durham. Ian McDonald, of the Department of Christian Ethics and Practical Theology at Edinburgh, joined the team after the first two meetings. Part I was drafted by me using notes taken at these consultations. Bruce Chilton who had contributed some very important input had to withdraw from the group at this stage to take up an appointment at Yale. Representatives of some of the projects in Part II attended a further two meetings at which the possibility and character of what has now emerged were discussed. Peter Sedgwick and Alan Suggate were responsible for following up individual projects and enlisting their cooperation. Ian McDonald drafted Part III as a response to and rounding off of Parts I and II.

We should make it clear what this little book is *not*. It does *not* attempt anything like a comprehensive survey of what the Gospels say about the kingdom of God. A different group, a longer time, and no doubt different emphases and insights would have emerged, which could have been more fully drawn out. We did in fact range more widely and dig more deeply at particular points. But the book is intended more as an example of what a small interdisciplinary group can do, rather than as a finished, rounded study. On the contrary we want it to be incomplete, to leave lines of thought undeveloped, aspects untouched, in the hope that it will stimulate and provoke others to pursue these thoughts and develop such aspects.

In the same way Part II is hardly intended to be a complete survey of all the ways that Christian churches, groups and individuals are responding to the social and spiritual needs of the North East. A good many other projects could and perhaps should be encouraged to express their objectives and hopes as a means of sharing, encouraging and challenging. Part II attempts simply to be representative and illustrative. The contributors, too, make no claims to provide blueprints for others, only examples of what might and can be done in particular circumstances. We are most grateful to them for their willing cooperation. No surprise should be expressed at the frequency with which unemployment is mentioned. That is the harshest social reality of the North East and if Part II helps bring that reality home to other regions of Britain it will have achieved one of its aims.

If it is not too presumptuous, we would like this little book to function as a sort of parable, the kind of parable Jesus told and lived – sometimes winning assent, sometimes surprising, sometimes stimulating further thought, sometimes provoking active response. Part I can perhaps be likened to one of Michelangelo's incomplete statues, with the face and form only beginning to emerge from the living stone, exciting observers to wonder how the finished work might appear. In Part II we kept editing to a minimum, hoping that the freshness of individual styles and comments will have their own impact. Not all would claim to be motivated by explicitly Christian concerns. But Jesus chose some unexpected examples in his parables. Part III is one person's response to the whole enterprise. We wholly expect that someone else's would be quite different. At least we hope so.

Candles and parables. To shed light and provoke response. We naturally would like this modest little effort to serve some useful purpose in British churches, presumably in study and house groups – helping their members to hear afresh something at least of Jesus' message of the kingdom and to ask what living in the light of the kingdom might mean for themselves and their fellowship groups. 'The kingdom of God is like . . .' Complete this sentence in word and life.

James D. G. Dunn
Durham, July 1986

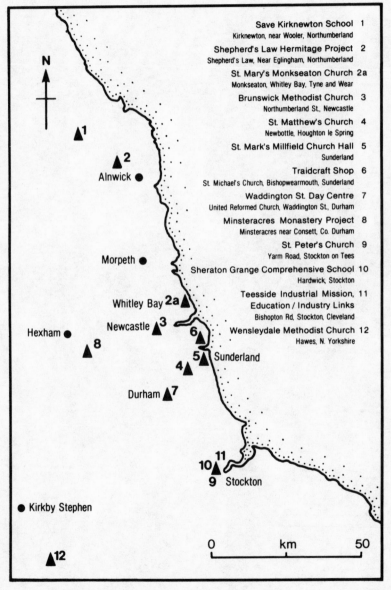

N

Save Kirknewton School 1
Kirknewton, near Wooler, Northumberland

Shepherd's Law Hermitage Project 2
Shepherd's Law, Near Eglingham, Northumberland

St. Mary's Monkseaton Church 2a
Monkseaton, Whitley Bay, Tyne and Wear

Brunswick Methodist Church 3
Northumberland St., Newcastle

St. Matthew's Church 4
Newbottle, Houghton le Spring

St. Mark's Millfield Church Hall 5
Sunderland

Traidcraft Shop 6
St. Michael's Church, Bishopwearmouth, Sunderland

Waddington St. Day Centre 7
United Reformed Church, Waddington St., Durham

Minsteracres Monastery Project 8
Minsteracres near Consett, Co. Durham

St. Peter's Church 9
Yarm Road, Stockton on Tees

Sheraton Grange Comprehensive School 10
Hardwick, Stockton

Teesside Industrial Mission, 11
Education / Industry Links
Bishopton Rd, Stockton, Cleveland

Wensleydale Methodist Church 12
Hawes, N. Yorkshire

▲1

▲2
Alnwick ●

Morpeth ●

Whitley Bay 2a▲

Newcastle ▲3

Hexham ● ▲8

6▲

4▲ 5▲ Sunderland

Durham ▲7

10▲11
9 Stockton

● Kirkby Stephen

0   km   50

▲12

PART I

What Meaning has 'the Kingdom of God' for Today?

1 | Introduction

This book had its beginning in a small group of Christian theologians who met in Durham for several days of discussion scattered between April and October 1985. We were drawn together by a simple, yet challenging question: What meaning has Jesus' talk of the kingdom of God for North-East England today? The basic conviction being, of course, that Jesus' teaching is of primary importance for Christians. It lies at the heart of Christianity, has had an incalculable influence on and through the churches down the centuries, and ought to be allowed to continue exercising that influence today. Meeting as Christians in the heartland of a part of the country notorious for its levels of unemployment and related social ills, we felt no need to apologise for asking the question.

As the question itself indicates, our concern was two-edged. First, to try to hear afresh the teaching of Jesus about the kingdom of God, in the hope that any answers which might emerge to the question should properly represent and re-express the message of Jesus. Second, to keep constantly in view the social reality which is North-East England today, in the hope that any answers which might emerge to the question should have something to say to that social reality.

These twin concerns are not so easily held together as some may think. In the past 'the kingdom of God' has been like a very

3

flexible rubber mould which individuals and groups have been able to pull into a variety of shapes. The resulting impression has often been a jumble of ideas drawn from within the Bible and beyond: the kingdom = the church; the kingdom = the missionary effort round the world; or again, the kingdom = the classless society; or the kingdom = the moral or economic utopia of some political party or sect. The danger of reading our own vision and ideals into 'the kingdom of God' is all too real. We were therefore resolved from the first that our discussion should be controlled by what the New Testament actually says regarding 'Jesus' talk of the kingdom of God'.

At the same time, it was clearly not enough simply to *describe* what the New Testament says about the kingdom. We could not assume that a message delivered to a first-century, largely agrarian, Palestinian society will be immediately and directly applicable to a twentieth-century North East suffering from the effects of long-term industrial decline. Theological reflection consists of (1) coming to terms with the strangeness and foreignness (to us) of that original message, (2) attempting to hear that message as far as possible in its original terms and with its original impact, and (3) re-expressing that message in equivalent terms and, hopefully, with the equivalent impact. The evidence of the New Testament therefore formed the basis but not the limit of our discussion. And the goal of 'meaning for North-East England' we tried to keep ever before us.

So the group's task was no easy one. The discussion frequently wandered back and forth as we struggled to keep both concerns before us. Nevertheless as we proceeded something of a sense of excitement grew in us, as we began to grasp and be grasped by some of the findings which emerged, or perhaps we may say, some of the insights which came to us. For these insights seemed to meet our double concern, to be both firmly rooted in Jesus' teaching and to have some potential relevance to our contemporary society.

The final task we set ourselves was to formulate and elaborate these findings or insights and to offer them for a wider circle. Our hope is that such potential as they have as a re-expression of Jesus' teaching about the kingdom of God may be realized in the North East today.

2 | The Kingdom of God in the Teaching of Jesus

1. A fundamental concept

God's kingdom has been and continues to be a basic element in Christian theology. The reason for this is simple: the kingdom of God was at the very centre of Jesus' own message. Although historical research has questioned whether a number of features of the Gospel tradition go back all the way to Jesus, the fact that Jesus preached the kingdom is regarded on all sides as a matter of virtual certainty.

The evidence of the Gospels is plain. Jesus was remembered as one who came preaching the kingdom of God (Matt. 4.17; Mark 1.15; Luke 4.43; John 3.3). When he sent out his disciples it was with the same central theme (Matt. 10.7; Luke 9.2). As a famed teller of parables, his largest group of parables begin, 'The kingdom of God is like . . .' (particularly Matt. 13). He evidently understood his ministry of healing, or at least of exorcism, in the same terms (Matt. 12.28; Luke 11.20). The first of his beatitudes likewise refers to the kingdom (Matt. 5.3; Luke 6.20).

If therefore the kingdom was so central in Jesus' preaching, it cannot lack importance for his followers.

What then was his message of the kingdom? What would it convey to his hearers? It seemed simplest to summarize our findings by asking three questions: *What* is the kingdom? *When* is the kingdom? *Where* is the kingdom?

5

2. What is the kingdom?

Two points became immediately clear to us.

(*a*) Jesus never defined or explained the phrase 'kingdom of God'. He must therefore have assumed that his hearers would understand what it was he was speaking of. In other words, the meaning of the phrase must have been either familiar or self-evident to his hearers. And since we today can compare it with related and similar uses of the time, we too can understand what Jesus meant.

(*i*) In the language used by Jesus (Aramaic), the word translated 'kingdom' had a broader range of meaning. It spoke more of kingship, the exercise of kingly rule, of reign more than domain. So the phrase 'kingdom of God' would probably be better translated 'God's kingly rule'.

(*ii*) In the translations (Targums) of the biblical Hebrew into the everyday Aramaic of Jesus' time the Hebrew was often interpreted and paraphrased. In the translation of Isa. 24.23 our phrase appears. The Hebrew text speaks of God ruling in the future:

> . . . the Lord of hosts will reign in Mount Zion.

In the Targum of Isaiah this promise becomes:

> . . . the kingdom of the Lord of hosts will be revealed on
> Mount Zion.

Obviously for the translator, to speak of 'the kingdom of God' was simply a way of speaking of God himself reigning. Jesus' hearers would probably have understood the phrase in the same way – 'the kingdom of God' as a way of speaking of God himself ruling over his own.

(*iii*) 'The kingdom of God' is therefore like a number of similarly constructed phrases – the glory of God, the spirit of God, the wisdom of God, and so on. All were well known to Jesus' contemporaries and all share the same character. They are ways of speaking about God in his active outreach to his creation and his people. They do not describe entities other than God, so much as God himself in creation, revelation and redemption.

For Jesus and his hearers therefore the phrase 'God's kingdom' would speak of God's reign, of his dynamic rule.

(*b*) When Jesus did say something descriptive about God's kingdom he regularly spoke in parables and metaphors. The

6

kingdom of God is like a woman using leaven to make bread; or like a man finding a pearl of great value and selling everything in order to buy it; and so on (Matt. 13). His exorcisms were in some sense a picture and expression of the kingdom (Matt. 12.28; Luke 11.20).

This tells us that for Jesus the kingdom was not simply a concept to be argued over, a piece of information to be passed on. It was something which could not be so much defined as illustrated. It was something which engaged the whole attention, like a fascinating story or a captivating action. Its meaning was not spelt out, but depended on how the parable was heard, how the healing was interpreted. And there were many who heard without understanding (Mark 4.10–12). Just as there were those who interpreted Jesus' exorcisms not as an expression of God's rule but of Satan's (Mark 3.22–30).

From these two preliminary conclusions a very important corollary follows. The kingdom is *God's*. This at once warns us against any notion that the kingdom can be identified with a human organization – even the human organization of the followers of Jesus. Talk today of 'building' the kingdom, of 'spreading' the kingdom (language often used in the dedication of a church collection) can be seriously misleading. It makes the kingdom sound like a social club or an expanding business; whereas Jesus intended to focus his hearers' minds on God himself.

To put it another way. God's kingdom is outside our power. It is not something we can control. It is not something we can reduce to a piece of paper or a plan of campaign. In theological language, the kingdom is always 'transcendent'; it lies beyond the limits of our ordinary knowledge and action. The kingdom is *God's*. It is God exercising his rule over what is his.

3. When is the kingdom?

This is a question which cannot be ignored, since it has caused a good deal of perplexity and debate among New Testament scholars. The problem is that Jesus seems to have spoken of God's kingdom as something yet to come in the future. But, at the same time, he evidently also spoke of it as already present or active through his ministry. We may consider, for example, on the one hand, the second petition of the Lord's prayer – 'May your kingdom come' (Matt. 6.10). To ask for the kingdom to come is to acknowledge that it is not yet here. On the other, compare Matt. 12.28 – 'If it is by the Spirit of God that I cast out demons, then the kingdom of God has come upon you'.

In one sense this was not so surprising. For the Jewish tradition in which Jesus stood could itself conceive of God's kingship over his creation here and now, especially over his people Israel (e.g. Ps. 44.4; Dan. 4.34–35), while also looking for that kingship to be fully exercised and acknowledged throughout creation (e.g. Isa. 24.23; Dan. 2.35,44).

But Jesus' teaching was nonetheless distinctive. For one thing, he stressed the nearness of this final rule – 'The kingdom of God is at hand' (Mark 1.15): 'There are some standing here who will not taste death before they see the kingdom of God come with power' (Mark 9.1). This was the main reason for the note of urgency so characteristic of his preaching: God stood ready to bring his royal rule into final effect, in a way which could only mean the end of this world as we know it. This 'eschatological' emphasis (from the Greek word 'eschaton' = end) is one which has been prominent in all discussions of Jesus' teaching throughout this century, and we found it impossible to ignore it or to play it down.

The other distinctive feature of Jesus' teaching on the kingdom was his assertion that this final rule of God was already to be seen in the present. It was not that he simply repeated the familiar Jewish theme – God as king of creation. That would have aroused no comment and would not have been particularly memorable. It was rather that he seems to have understood his own ministry as an expression or vehicle of that full and final rule over men and things. This is explicit in his exorcisms (Matt. 12.28; Mark 3.27) and implicit in the link he evidently saw between the kingdom imagery of a banquet and his own table fellowship (Luke 14.12–24; Matt. 22.2–10).

Such observations pose many questions and set many trains of thought in motion. We felt it most appropriate to focus on two.

(a) Jesus neither removed God's rule to the edge of human affairs, nor located it completely in their midst. He saw God's kingly rule as active in his own mission: its power could be experienced now; the quality of its relationships could be enjoyed in the present. But it could not be identified with anything in the present; it was yet to come in its full reality. Life could be lived already in the light of the coming kingdom, but life in the kingdom, society solely under the rule of God was not yet.

(b) When we looked at the ministry of Jesus as a whole, including his death and resurrection, this line of thought became still more challenging. The God who stands over against history, ready to wind up history, was already active in and through the history of Jesus. And that includes his suffering and crucifixion. God was in Christ not just in miracle and feasting but in his rejection and his shameful tortured death. God's exercise of his kingly rule came to its most emphatic expression not by exempting Jesus from that pain and humiliation, but through raising him from the dead – a manifestation of his power which could only come *through* suffering and death and on the other side of death.

4. *Where is the kingdom?*

All that has been so far said seems long ago and far removed from the circumstances and concerns of twentieth-century England. Jesus no longer walks among us. Nearly two thousand years have passed since he first proclaimed the kingdom's nearness. Yet it would be a mistake to tie Jesus' talk of the kingdom to his physical presence or to confine its present-future emphasis to a particular sequence of events in first-century Palestine. For Jesus said other things about the kingdom which cannot be so easily classified and safely shut up in the past. The almost timeless quality of so many of Jesus' parables, including 'the kingdom parables', should warn us against thinking of the kingdom and its coming in strict chronological terms.

In this area several key ideas came home with increasing force in our discussion – though, no doubt, had our discussions been extended, other points would have emerged as well. They can be grouped under three headings.

(a) *The unexpectedness of the kingdom.* A repeated feature of Jesus' teaching about the kingdom is the element of *surprise*. The kingdom of God belongs to the poor, not to the well-to-do (Luke 6.20). The least in the kingdom is greater than John the Baptist, himself the greatest man born (Matt. 11.11). Whoever does not receive the kingdom as a child will by no means enter it (Mark 10.14). The kingdom of heaven is like an employer who paid his workers the same wage even though some had worked eight time

9

as long as others (Matt. 20.1–16). Taxcollectors and harlots enter the kingdom before the righteous (Matt. 21.31).

One parable we considered at some length was that given in Mark 4.26–29:

> The kingdom of God is as a man scatters seed on the earth, and sleeps and wakes night and day. But the seed sprouts and grows, how he does not know. The earth produces, as of itself, first the blade, then the ear, then the full grain in the ear. When the yield appears, however, immediately he puts in the sickle, because the harvest has come.

What struck us was that the kingdom is likened to the whole process, not to any particular element within it – *not* to the seed, or the farmer, or the soil. Rather it is a parable of co-operation – farmer, seed, soil, all involved in harmonious interaction. What is surprising about it is the *ordinariness* of the whole process. Part of the image of the kingdom is the farmer going to bed, sleeping and getting up in the ordinary circle of daily activity – not really understanding the 'how' of the process in which he is involved.

The surprise of the kingdom, then, includes the challenging and reversal of what have become accepted values – both social and religious values. It includes too the recognition that the humdrum and ordinary can also illustrate and metaphor God's kingly rule. To hear Jesus' word of the kingdom is to become aware of unexpected realities and possibilities even in the ordinary and in what otherwise seem to be quite negative situations.

(b) *Responding to the kingdom.* So much of Jesus' teaching about the kingdom includes an emphasis on *response.* 'The kingdom of God is at hand: repent!' (Mark 1.15). 'Unless you turn and become like children, you will never enter the kingdom of heaven' (Matt. 18.3). The kingdom is something to be sought (Matt. 6.33), to be entered into (Mark 9.47; 10.23; etc.). It calls for preparation and for decisive action (Matt. 25.1–12; 13.44–46; Luke 9.62). It may even be a motive for leaving home and family (Luke 18.29).

In the parable of the farmer, seed and soil (Mark 4.26–29), the farmer seems to do nothing for most of the time. The seed grows, of itself, until harvest. But when harvest comes the seed does not reap 'of itself'. The farmer must be quick with his sickle, or the opportunity of ripe grain will pass him by. Without his response, the picture of the kingdom, and the reality of the kingdom which it expresses, would be incomplete.

Another parable focusses on the theme of forgiveness (Matt. 18.23–35). The kingdom of heaven is like a king who forgives a huge debt, but who then applies the full rigour of the law when the forgiven servant refuses to forgive a fellow servant. The kingdom includes both aspects. The one condition which God makes for his forgiveness to be experienced is the readiness to forgive.

Jesus speaks of God's royal power ready to break in upon our human situations. All it may await is our response. He speaks of God's power already at work in and through our everyday situations, where what is required is our readiness to discern when to wake and sleep and when to act. He speaks of God's kingdom in terms of human relationships where the key is forgiveness – so simple, but so difficult.

(c) *The kingdom and community*. Many of Jesus' words about the kingdom were about individuals – sowing, finding treasure, discovering a pearl, and so on. But in others he emphasized the importance of a *communal* dimension. It is implicit even in the parable of the farmer, the seed and the soil (Mark 4), where co-operation is a keynote, and the invitation is to recognize and play your part in co-operation with others. It is explicit in the parable about forgiveness (Matt. 18). Without reconciliation between individuals who should be colleagues, the message of forgiveness turns into one of judgment. Discerning the kingdom in a situation includes recognizing where God's judgment stands over an enterprise or a relationship, includes the appropriate repentance, includes the receiving and offering of forgiveness.

The same emphasis comes out in Jesus' imagery of the banquet for the kingdom and in his corresponding practice of table fellowship (Luke 14). In its openness to Pharisee, to taxcollector and sinner, to the poor and disadvantaged, Jesus' table-fellowship not only expressed a vision of the kingdom yet to be, but brought the reality of the kingdom in its reconciling power into present experience. Nor should we forget that in Matt. 25.31–46 Jesus extended the notion of God's kingship to include the demand that such concern should include the wider circle of the world's poor and disadvantaged.

Central to all this is the key insight that human relationship and community can be expressive of the kingdom of God when that relationship and community is open to the kingly rule of God. A mature relationship or community is one where 'Sorry' is said when necessary, and where forgiveness can be freely offered and received. And so often the trigger to that is the childlike recognition that we each need the forgiveness of God, since it is often the opening of ourselves to God's forgiveness which enables us to open ourselves to our neighbour. No wonder then that Jesus said 'You are not far from the kingdom' to the one who recognized that loving God with all one's being and loving one's neighbour as oneself hang together at the top of God's priorities (Mark 12.32–34). And perhaps the relationship of the second petition in each half of the Lord's prayer is more than accidental: God's kingdom comes when our sins are forgiven as we forgive the sins of others (Matt. 6.10,12).

'Surprise, response, community' – these three themes seemed to us to capture at least something of the 'where' of the kingdom. They formed three of the principal emphases which we drew from the Gospels and which we sought to bring into interaction with the issues and questions confronting us in North-East England today.

3 | God's Rule and North-East England Today

The other part of our task was to relate our findings to the reality of North-East England in the last decades of the twentieth century. Not that our discussion proceeded in such an orderly manner. Rather it zig-zagged back and forth as we tried to maintain a sort of dialogue with the biblical text – our own experience and concerns posing questions to the biblical text and in turn being challenged by the text and forced to reformulate our questions, and so on. In attempting to set down our reflections, however, it seemed more sensible to draw together our findings from the Gospels before going on to the trickier phase of bringing them into interaction with the social, economic and political needs and opportunities of the North East today.

Much of our discussion focussed on two issues – the relation of the kingdom to society, and the role of the church within that relationship.

1. Kingdom and society

At its simplest the problem can be defined thus: Is the kingdom in any sense a vision for society (or in larger terms, of creation)? Clearly if images like the banquet parables of Jesus have any relevance at this point (or in larger terms, a vision like Isa. 11.6–9), the answer must be Yes.

But that merely pushes the problem one step forward. For the question then becomes: (*a*) Is the kingdom a vision of society as we might hope for it to become within the history of humankind? Or (*b*) is it a vision of what only God can bring about and only will bring about in a wholly new stage of human existence (after the coming again of Christ, or after the resurrection, or in a new heaven and new earth, etc.)?

(*a*) The attractiveness of the first alternative is that it makes it easier to define an ethical, social, political role for the church as a whole and for individual Christians. It becomes a *Christian* responsibility to work to achieve that kind of society – and that would almost certainly mean active engagement in political programmes of social reform and improvement.

The *danger* of this option is equally apparent – the danger that we *identify* a *particular* social and political order with the kingdom and narrow the church's (and individual Christians') political role to that of a particular political option or a particular political party. The danger, in other words, of *confusing* the kingdom with particular political or social ethical objectives.

This option was open to Jesus too. But it is clear that he did not take it. He refused to provide a blueprint for social organization such as the Pharisees or the Essenes offered. The Pharisees saw it as their responsibility to live daily life as though the whole country was the temple; so they lived in accordance with the ritual purity required for the temple priests. The Essenes at the Qumran community beside the Dead Sea went even further and organized themselves in an even stricter application of the same principle. But Jesus rejected that option in favour of much more open-ended relationships, open to the religiously and socially unacceptable as well as others.

He also refused the option of trying to offer a political programme for his people. The Zealots did that as they worked from the principle that God alone was their king, and therefore they must resist the overlordship of the Roman occupying armies – by force. Jesus' counsel to give Caesar what was Caesar's due and to 'Love your enemy' (Mark 12.17; Matt. 5.44) was a complete rejection of the only live political option before a low-born Galilean who objected to the *status quo*.

Here our earlier findings spoke clearly. As soon as we see God's kingdom as something *we* bring about, and forget that it is *God's*, that it is God himself exercising his kingly rule, we have lost the way. As soon as we forget that the kingdom is *eschatological*, something which cannot be contained within the limits of this age without bringing it completely to an end, we have lost the way. As soon as we forget the unseen and *unexpected* character of the kingdom which surprises and disrupts and overturns the accepted patterns, we have lost the way. In short, if we have understood Jesus' teaching on the kingdom aright, any attempt to define the kingdom in terms of a specific programme of action (religious, social or political) has already lost sight of what Jesus said about the kingdom.

(*b*) The strength of the second alternative is that it prevents any such identification and maintains the recognition of the kingdom as a critical ideal by which all human systems (religious as well as social and political) need to be judged. Jesus apparently never spoke about the kingdom without thereby forcing his hearers to take a hard look at themselves in the light of what he said.

The *danger* of this option is that it can foster various kinds of irresponsibility. If the kingdom is God's and he will bring it into operation at some future time, then we ourselves need take no responsibility for the defects of the *status quo* or indeed for sustaining and supporting the better (or worse) features of the *status quo*. In other words, such an emphasis on the kingdom all too easily results in a passive or quietist attitude to social issues which resigns the whole business to God to sort out in the sweet by and by. Let's get back to our hymn-singing.

This option was open to Jesus too. There were then, as now, groups who sought simply a quiet life in which they could wait for God's deliverance. But Jesus refused to follow that route too. He went about proclaiming not so much the kingdom's future – a distant threat of a day of judgment at the far end of history. He proclaimed rather its *nearness*. Individuals and social institutions stood under threat of God's kingly rule soon to break in upon them. But he also saw the kingdom as already breaking in and mirrored in familiar events and situations. He called for *response* to his message of the kingdom and saw that response as part of the kingdom's coming. He saw in the human relationships of *forgiveness* and the acceptance of the meal table an expression of what should be and will be when God's will is done on earth as in heaven.

If then Jesus refused the options of identifying the kingdom with a particular religious, social and political order, or of separating the kingdom completely from the current religious, social and political order, how can we summarize the relation between kingdom and society as he saw it?

The answer seems to be that Jesus pointed to a middle way between these options. On the one hand he refused to offer a blueprint or programme for society. He used symbols and parables which individually and together do not build up into a comprehensive picture of society. On the other hand, his parables, drawn immediately from contemporary society, and his metaphors, lived out in the midst of his own society, provided repeated challenge to the attitudes and practices of that social, religious and political order.

In short, we will not get far in our enterprise until we realize that it is not possible to define the kingdom in any extensive way. We cannot even say that Jesus himself had a fully rounded vision of society as it should and will be under God's reign. But we can see how Jesus spoke and lived his message of the kingdom in terms of a sequence of individual metaphors and parables, all of which called in one way or another for a practical response in a whole sequence of personal and social relationships. And we can say that this response was a fundamental part of his vision of the kingdom. By *living* the kingdom in a whole sequence of concrete situations remembered in the Gospels, Jesus brought the kingly rule of God to expression.

2. Kingdom, society and church

What then may we say is the role of the church in relation to the kingdom and society? – that is, the role both of individual Christians and of Christians in their own social grouping for worship and mission.

One inviting option is to identify the church with the kingdom – the church as the kingdom of God on earth. But that will not do, any more than it will do to identify the kingdom with some political programme. The kingdom of God, God ruling as he would, always stands over against us in judgment, in calling us to repentance – the church as much as any other social organization belonging to this age. Once we let slip the character of the kingdom in its power continually to challenge us afresh, we have lost sight of the kingdom of which Jesus spoke. That will remain true for all, followers of Jesus or not. The kingdom of God in Jesus' message always escapes final definition and retains its transcendent quality and capacity to surprise and upset our safe patterns, to criticize and call in question, to provoke and summon to ever new response.

But if we may not identify the kingdom with the church, neither may we simply lump the church with society as standing wholly over against the kingdom. For the church is by definition those who are seeking to respond to Jesus' message of the kingdom, and, if we are right, even that response is itself part of the kingdom. If not yet the community where forgiveness is freely given and received and mutual acceptance in open-ended friendship is universally practised, at least the church is the body of people who recognize that that is the way it should be.

All that we have reflected on so far suggests that the church's role in relation to kingdom and society is to be a messenger of the kingdom in more or less the way that Jesus was. That will mean at least two things.

(a) The church's message of the kingdom should take its pattern from Jesus. That is to say, it should use symbols and metaphors and tell stories as Jesus did – including not least Jesus' own stories (parables) and the story of Jesus' own life and ministry, to challenge hearers (church as well as society at large) to respond and live in a way appropriate to these symbols and stories.

(b) The church in its own life should itself seek to live in response to these symbols and stories in such a way as to show that they are not hopelessly idealistic or unrealistic. What is the equivalent today of Jesus' exorcisms which brought the kingdom among men? What is the equivalent of his table-fellowship which imaged the banquet of the new age of God's final rule? Such a life cannot be lived in isolation from society, even if it refuses to take its norms and values from that society. Such a life may end as his ended – in misunderstanding, in rejection, in death. But that too may be God's way of exercising his kingly rule.

This train of thought led us naturally to cast about for examples of this kind of speaking and living the kingdom in North East England today. As Jesus drew his examples from contemporary society, so we began to seek out symbols and stories of contemporary Christian involvement which might have something of the effect of Jesus' stories and life. A well known saying came home to us over and again: 'Better to light a candle than to rail at the darkness.' So we began to ask, What candles are there in the North East whose light may be an inspiration and challenge to others?

The next stage of our inquiry therefore was to contact a number of projects, various in kind, and to ask them to share with us something of their own vision, its theological rationale and meaning. Twelve responded. Their responses follow in no particular order.

PART II

Responding to the Kingdom

4 | Response to the Kingdom

RAY SKINNER

Spirituality – the importance of space

Having grown up in the South of England, one of the main attractions of the North East of England is that it is not far from the 'desert', i.e. wide open spaces such as the Pennines and Cheviots. It was a high priority for my wife and myself to have a tiny cottage, in fact up near Greenhead, which we owned for ten years. Unfortunately, with a growing family it became harder to get to it, without a lot of preparation. We decided the funds tied up in it could be better used elsewhere, so we sold it two years ago. It was important, however, to both of us, to know that it was there: even if only in our minds, we could stand back from either inner city Newcastle where we were for five years, or our present mining parish where we have been for nearly ten years; it gave us the all important other perspective we look for.

At the beginning of his Gospel St Mark gives, in summary, examples of what the coming of the kingdom means to Jesus, expressing his relationship to his father God; the healing of various diseases and casting out demons, for many people (the whole city? Mark 1.33) as well as preaching and teaching. But the summary is preceded by the stark record of Jesus' wilderness experience, one which he regularly returns to. Our experience of the kingdom needs such a perspective.

21

Training/employment in the North East

Eight years ago, my Parochial Church Council decided to sponsor a Youth Opportunities Programme, and set up a trust (in an association with my old parish in Elswick, Newcastle). We purchased a large Miners' Welfare Hall, which became the base for twenty-five trainees, in a production-based training workshop. The YOP changed to the Youth Training Scheme, and we changed with it, all the time sharing the ultimate financial responsibility for the scheme. Early this year (1985), however, as MSC were cutting down nationally the number of places for our kind of scheme, they withdrew from the building. Learning from experience with this project, for the last five years I have been actively involved in the development of a Youth Business Initiative Scheme, which seeks to support young people in starting their own business. Now our own building is available for start-up enterprises.

The biblical theology undergirding this work is drawn (1) from an understanding of the Hebrew concept 'Shalom' – humanity being created for wholeness, realizing the full potential for which individuals were created within society; and (2) from a basic understanding of Jesus' ministry being a balance between preaching and healing. Given, as public opinion polls etc. confirm, that the number one problem our society faces is unemployment, we, as Christians, clearly have an obligation to offer healing at the deepest of perceived human needs. However, the preaching/healing model has led us as a church to recognize the need for an explicit statement of what the gospel is, alongside an implicit healing ministry; hence the recognition by my church leaders, that evangelism must go alongside a healing ministry. Hence their support of my being co-ordinating secretary for Mission England in the North East. (So far we have been able to achieve less in the field of evangelism within our Parish than we would have liked!).

Third World involvement

My wife and I came to this parish, having already been involved in the beginnings of a trading company with the explicit objective of working for justice in world trade relations, as understood from a biblical perspective. The parish support us in this, and a few parishioners work full time for Traidcraft. As its nominal chairman, I do what little I can to support the staff, now nearly a hundred, working from our Gateshead factory, themselves supporting thousands of third world jobs, in this crucial field of Christian mission. The theology behind this is again 'Shalom'.

I am increasingly concerned to work out, in a way that can be put simply and clearly, the relation between this world as part of God's world, and what I have been privileged to share in here in the North East. I do not like the lemming philosophy which seems to suggest that the problems our world faces can be left to Christ to sort out when he returns on the clouds of heaven (no doubt associated with a final holocaust). On the other hand, neither do I like the tendency of modern theology to suggest that humankind can work it all out on its own. Of considerable influence upon me has been the commentary on the book of Revelation by G. B. Caird; here Caird concludes time and time again that God gives us another chance, but it would twist New Testament theology beyond breaking point to suggest that there will *not* be a time when Christ returns. Is not the kingdom above all about relationship with God in Christ, in this world at the same time as in heaven? But this has implications for speaking intelligently about this world as part of a greater cosmos which God rules, and if your group gets there before I do, then good luck to you!

5 | Kirknewton School – Our Campaign for its Retention

HELEN BLOWERS

The small village of Kirknewton, together with Westnewton and the surrounding area of the College Valley (near Wooler in Northumberland), has a sparse population. It is a rugged, beautiful place, almost entirely given over to hill farming; and indeed the majority of the adult population work on the land as farmers, stockmen and upland shepherds. St Gregory's Church serves the second largest parish (Church of England) in the country and there has been a church school in the village for over a hundred years – the present school being built in 1964 for twenty-five pupils up to the age of eleven. These numbers dropped by almost one third when the three-tier education system was brought in by the county, and last year the roll was at an all-time low of nine pupils.

The school has always played an important part in the life of this community. It is a friendly, welcoming place where people can meet, not only when picking up their children but also at the open days and coffee evenings organized by the staff and the Friends of the School. The school has always taught its children that they have a part to play in the life of their community, and the instilling of this solid sense of their own identity and feelings of consideration for others, their community responsibility, stands them in good stead when they move on to Middle and High School. The community contributes much to the school: it takes a great interest in the progress of its young, for the existence of the school gives the older people a belief in the continuing life of their village. The children feel cherished, and learn to give a great deal in time, thought and deed to the community in so many different ways.

I attended many different schools as a child (I come from an Air Force family) – both church and council. Although there was no real difference in the academic curriculum, even as a child I could sense the difference in atmosphere between the two types of school. There was a loving kindness, a feeling of security and wholeness which to me seemed lacking at the council schools I attended. As a child, I could not have put into words what this difference was, but I certainly felt it, and thrived at those church schools in a way I never did at the others. What I *do* know is that I perceived the church, the school, the teachers and the vicar as one complete unit. This same care for the *whole* of the individual – not just for intellectual and physical development but for spiritual growth too – this complete nurturing is what I, as a member of the local church, want for the children of our community. I want each child to learn that, in the eyes of God, he is unique and precious, and that his best friend, his teacher, his worst enemy – and the old lady across the road – are equally special.

On a narrower level, the religious education that our children receive at Kirknewton school is the only introduction and guide to Christianity that some of them will get, since we live in an increasingly secular society. The faithful must surely see it not only as a right but as a duty to fight for the retention of such schools. They are needed today more than ever.

Last autumn we discovered that our school was to be closed. We decided to fight because we knew with absolute certainty its closure would do our children no good, nor the life of our rural community.

We fought because, win or lose, the alternative to fighting was unacceptable. We could not have lived comfortably with the knowledge that we just stood back and did nothing to prevent an authority taking from a community something so dearly held – 'Tis better to have loved and lost. . . .'

We fought because we were not prepared to have 'experts' tell all and sundry their preconceived notions of what made our community tick, to have them declare, unchallenged, that they knew what was best for us and our children – all this without bothering to talk to us! We fought because we were not having educational theory – dogma, if you like – take precedence over what we knew to be right for our children.

I fought because I believe passionately in the reality of local democracy, and because I was not prepared to allow the Jeremiahs in our midst to convince us that campaigning for retention would be a futile exercise, as the powers that be had long since made up their minds to close our school, and nothing anyone might say or do would change that. For me, then, it became a need to save our school, not just for its own sake, but to prove beyond any doubt that the opinions and needs of the individual, the small group, the rural community, are precious. They *matter*, and they *will* be heeded by those who make the decisions. They must, however, be expressed loud and clear to those authorities. To refuse to fight for something worthwhile because you convince yourself that there is little possibility of winning, to fail to voice opinion when it is clearly called for, and then to declare with a peculiar satisfaction 'I told you so!' when that something *is* lost, must surely be perverse. To me, it was anathema.

So we campaigned. We bombarded the local media with news, petitioned, toured with an information tent, walked several body-aching sponsored miles, cajoled, threatened, produced a good document stating our case (if I say so as shouldn't!), raged, laughed and prayed. I do believe that God guided us in our campaign from the very start, and enabled us to use our various talents to the full. There were bleak times: the nights I spent re-writing our document in despair, convinced that it was trite, unbelievable and fit only for the bin; the gloom which threatened to swamp me whenever one of the (fortunately few) 'knockers' told us yet again that we were wasting our time. Perhaps the worst day of all was when we learnt that the Director of Education had indeed recommended closure to the Councillors.

But the ups *always* came after the downs. There was the visit to our school by members of the Education Committee, and there was the change, perceptible to us all, in the attitudes of many of these Councillors once they were able to see for themselves just what it was that we were determined to save and why. The truth,

27

the validity of our campaign, could not be gainsaid – this was marvellous and exciting for us to see.

There was the woman who said, after the campaign was over, 'I'm sorry. I didn't help as much as I ought' – but she did. She constantly encouraged when the sceptics sneered, when I fleetingly wondered, treacherously, if it was worth all the hassle and the disruption to family life. We wondered whether we were really doing the best for our children by trying to keep such a small school when the experts were telling us our children might be educationally disadvantaged if they did not transfer to a bigger school. She never doubted the rightness of our cause, she refused to accept that it was lost before it was even begun. Surely a wonderful example of ministry, and a lesson to be learnt, by me any way, that words of encouragement, praise and love should never be stinted.

Our campaign resulted in a success more total than even the most optimistic amongst us had dared dream of. For the Councillors were unanimous in their view that the school must stay and continue to serve the community with excellence. ('A victory for kindness and common sense!', I burbled to the waiting press as we wafted out of the committee room on cloud nine.)

We are floating gently earthwards now, delighting in the day-to-day running of our school, and the knowledge that a community has forged and reforged links that will surely never be lost. We have had restored to us not just the future of our school, but also the knowledge of the worth of our views. We have regained belief in ourselves.

6 | Rural Evangelism

GORDON GATWARD

I see the kingdom of God in terms of Jesus being Lord and exerting his rule both globally and individually, which means in a personal level accepting his rule over, in and through my own life and ministry. Therefore, I have to consider all I do and am in the light of this knowledge and experience. My life must be subject to his rule, guidance, teaching and living presence, and how I see and what I do in this world must come under that same scrutiny. Christ is Lord. This means I see him as such in all areas of life, and endeavour to make this real for others in sharing with them the joys and challenges of the kingdom, i.e. the experience of accepting the Lordship of Jesus over their lives. This must entail an awareness of his saving role in terms of his being able to forgive and wipe out sin, but also includes the co-operative work with him in seeing and making this world as he intends it to be – to spread love, healing and goodness, and to treat all aspects of his creation with the respect, sympathy, dignity and delight for which they were intended. Thus, there can be no separation between my concept of the kingdom and my understanding of ministry. The two belong together.

The ministry to which I believe I have been called is that of the rural church, partly through my own rural upbringing, but largely through my conviction that this is where God wants me. For the past few years this has been in the communities of upper

29

Wensleydale (North Yorkshire), communities largely dependent on tourism and farming, small, tightly knit and remote from any large urban centres. These characteristics of the area are frequently seen as problems, yet in terms of ministry they can be strengths. For example, in these communities it is possible to become involved in many areas of local life, and also to have contact with the majority of people who live in the area, so enabling one to offer both the gospel and the ministry of Christ's church. In terms of my own experience this has led to close involvement with local agriculture, as I have made it a regular practice to visit the Auction Mart, the local Farmers' Discussion Group, and many local farms. Such contacts frequently lead to pastoral care, and often develop into situations where such issues as the environment and modern farming practices are discussed in the light of the gospel. I have also joined the local Fell Rescue Team, regularly visit the village schools and old folks' clubs, and I run the youth club in Hawes itself. In addition, I share in the chaplaincy work at a small hospital for the mentally handicapped in a nearby village, and with two local vicars I work a regular hospital visiting rota to all those from the area who have been hospitalized. All of these situations lead to many opportunites, not only to offer a caring ministry but also on a personal level to speak of Jesus. These areas are not seen purely as my domain, however; the work is shared wherever possible with other members of the church and is supported by them in prayer. The ministry is not one man, but the whole Body of Christ working together. This has been illustrated in the Methodist Circuit recently by the growing concern for evangelism, and the recognition that the whole church must see this as its primary aim. Over recent months one congregation has hosted a student mission led by students from Cliff College (Derbyshire). They then organized their own Children's Mission led by their own Sunday School staff. As a Circuit we borrowed the local Auction Mart for an evening and used the sheep ring for a very effective evangelistic meeting. Since then a group has been established in the Circuit to meet regularly for prayer and sharing, with regard to learning more of God's will for us in the Dale.

Besides agriculture, tourism is the other main source of income in the Dale, and this again offers new areas of ministry which we are at the moment just beginning to explore. So far, it has led to a number of projects and ventures being started from an Outdoor

Pursuits Centre in the nearby village of Askrigg. This was inspired and built through the vision and efforts of the then vicar, and led to my own involvement with groups of young people who have camped in the Dale and asked me to serve as their chaplain and outdoor activities leader. In Hawes we have also established a programme that takes place weekly during the summer holidays called 'Discover the Dale'. This is run on an ecumenical basis and takes place in the Methodist Church. Either the vicar or I welcome the visitors and introduces the speaker, who then deals with some particular aspect of Dales life. These evenings have proved popular and effective in that we normally attract an audience of a hundred to a hundred and fifty people. Many of these having found a warm welcome in the church on a Tuesday evening then come along on the Sunday and share in worship.

Talking about the people who visit the Dale raises another issue which we have tried to deal with locally. Due to the pressures of farming and the tourist trade, we have found that many local youngsters do not get away for a family holiday. A few years ago the Circuit responded to this by organizing holidays for local children and young people. Again these have proved very successful and during the past summer approximately eighty youngsters went on the holidays organized in Blackpool and the Lake District by the Circuit youth leaders.

The writer Francis Schaeffer has described people in terms of their being like a portrait of God which has been defaced by the mud of sin. That mud has to be removed so that the Creator's image can shine through, and so that they can not only recognize their Creator but also see their Creator's likeness in themselves. When this happens they discover and experience Jesus as Lord. In all that we are doing and trying to do here in Wensleydale, this is our aim.

7 | *Waddington Street Day Centre*

JUDY BANISTER

The Waddington Street Day Centre was started four years ago in response to the need to provide day care for the mentally ill in the community. It is run by a group of voluntary helpers drawn largely from local churches and is held in the Waddington Street United Reformed church hall, which is conveniently situated in the centre of Durham City.

Initially we met for one day in the week, but within a few months decided to open for a second day. Currently we meet on Monday and Thursday from 10.00 a.m. until 3.30 p.m., and about sixty members attend, some one day a week, some two days, and a few slightly less frequently. Members are usually referred from the County (Psychiatric) Hospital or Social Services, though a small number have come through other contacts. Most have a long history of mental illness and fairly regular hospital admissions.

Concerning what actually goes on in the Centre I should like to quote from an article written by one of our members:

In the Centre there is a relaxed, informal atmosphere with no set routine or programme of events. Members do what they feel like doing, although there are occasionally organised activities, such as relaxation, games, visits to the swimming baths or places of interest. On the whole, however, most people prefer to sit and chat over a cup of tea or coffee, perhaps play card

33

games, scrabble, darts or dominoes, or take advantage of materials provided for handicrafts, such as knitting, embroidery, basketry, stool-making, oil painting, macrame, rug making, etc. Lunch is provided for a small charge and members help prepare the meal and wash up. During the summer coach outings were arranged and a good time had by all.

Since that was written more than twelve months ago there have been several new developments. A psychologist from the hospital now comes each Monday morning to take a group therapy session. We have a pottery class on Thursday afternoons, a poetry group meets, a choir is supposed to be being formed (we are somewhat short of sopranos!), and it is hoped that we might have a 'faith group' where members can discuss their beliefs (or lack of them). We also hold a fortnightly meeting for all members of the Centre, so that everyone has an opportunity to voice their comments, suggestions and complaints.

Some of us also meet together each week (not on a Centre day) to give thanks and to pray for the work of the Centre. We are anxious not to lose sight of our vision of Christ the Lord ruling over the Centre, a vision which we have shared from the beginning and of which we have often reminded each other. We should otherwise be tempted to despair, for we can feel helpless in the face of depression and mental illness and overwhelmed by feelings of inadequacy and failure, when, as has happened twice this year, we have been faced with suicide, the ultimate cry of despair. And so we are driven to prayer; we know that the love of Jesus can help our people and help free them from the darkness which destroys their lives and prevents them achieving the potential that still lies within them. And, in spite of failures and difficulties, it has been our privilege to see exciting growth. From the beginning we found an extraordinarily large measure of acceptance and tolerance among the members.

Almost all felt rejected by society on account of being mentally ill, and this common experience resulted in a ready-made bond between them, but gradually we have seen acceptance and tolerance become fellowship and love. When we sit at lunch together we sit as a family; when news reached us that one member had killed himself there was a spontaneous desire to go into church together and to commit him into God's safe keeping, and we sat, not scattered around the church, but together as a family.

As love and care and concern for each other have spread we have seen, albeit with setbacks, individuals strengthened and growing, and finally we have had the joy of seeing some of them acknowledging and responding to Christ's love, and in spite of the enormity of some of the problems we continue growing. 'We belong to that kingdom which cannot be shaken.'

8 | To Work or Not to Work, That is the Question

BILL WRIGHT

While on the staff of St John's College, Durham, Dr John Cumpstey spent a couple of years working with laypeople from Teesside Industrial Mission, and taught us a lot about the church's role in a changing society.

The church has four key tasks:

1. An evangelistic role: to enable and sustain Christian conviction – to 'make' Christians, to bring people to Christ;

2. A pastoral role: to serve *everyone*, without exception, members and non-members, for their own sakes – in their individual needs and in their corporate situations too (in their marriage breakdowns but also when they make a thousand workers redundant);

3. A prophetic role: to be creatively critical of the world as we find it;

4. To develop a partnership in ministry *in the secular world* between laity and clergy.

That turned out to be the most practical theological input I ever received from anyone and I thank God for it. Two decades ago, John Cumpstey spent months helping us apply it to *work*, preparing us, no doubt, for the crisis now upon us.

The way we work is changing in revolutionary fashion. Many of our manufacturing industries have collapsed for good; recently arrived light industries have now decamped as branch firms have closed; service industries have shrunk too; high tech developments have shunned the North East; a quarter of our people do not work at all while the rest fight for overtime; not only does the South get richer while the North gets poorer, but within the North, the gulf widens between working and workers; retirements begin at fifty; unemployment lasts for years and years; job splitting and sharing emerges; regular retraining is the norm; sabbaticals are appearing; government schemes replace 'real jobs' for almost all our young people; even graduates cannot expect a job any longer; married women join their husbands in expecting to work across most of a life time, and even compete against their sons and daughters for scarce jobs; people seem glad to be offered firm contracts for as little as six months' employment; basic working weeks reduce and holidays expand. Either we force a quarter of our people into prolonged demoralizing unemployment, or we continue the process of sharing out whatever work is available among *all* the folk available to do it, inevitably in smaller quantities. (Stockton-Darlington Railway drivers worked over seventy hours a week in 1825! We have just about halved that by 1985.)

Industrial Mission, working closely with a growing number of congregations, is already in the vanguard of experimentation, trying to discover more appropriate patterns of work for the North East: chaplains and laypeople together thinking and planning creatively; running risks with property and finance; moving into completely uncharted areas; discovering all kinds of allies outside our congregations; facing the very grim reality of our economic situation squarely, and building up an inter-linking network of hopeful activity and positive debate.

Let me briefly describe what is going on:

We are *researching the nature of our work-revolution* as carefully as we can. We want to know precisely what the trends are and in particular whether we are merely in deep recession or permanent de-industrialization. That is a vital political debate which the major parties still cannot face yet.

We are bringing *educationalists and employers/trade unionists* together to rethink what we must teach young people who no longer have traditional types of work waiting for them at sixteen. Stimulating curriculum changes are already emerging out of these

38

interchanges. Education has become too important to leave to teachers alone.

We are *writing and sharing disturbing ideas* and getting these widely discussed in congregations and among politicians at all levels. We have made practical proposals to Cabinet ministers about help they could give to voluntary bodies willing to put new ideas to the test and new energies into the search.

We are using Manpower Services Commission finance to develop projects under the Youth Training Scheme, Community Programme and Voluntary Projects Programme, and are thus able to see both the strengths and the weaknesses of *government job creation* schemes and to help improve them through central groups like Church Action with the Unemployed.

We are finding skills and commitment from experienced laypeople, and finance from churches, business, local government and Manpower Services Commission, *to explore 'real job' creation* through a decades-long plan to develop self-employment, especially among young people in school and immediately afterwards. We are also keen to help people working in the black economy to get the business skills necessary to set up legitimate businesses.

We have been closely associated with company *early retirement schemes* and with the increasing urge to *split or share jobs*, not least when these involve making opportunities for young people.

We are realistic enough to know that tens of thousands of people will not benefit from any of the above experiments and will remain unemployed for large chunks of a normal working life. We have set up centres where they can determine their own *future-without-paid-work* creatively and without stigma.

We spend a lot of time questioning our current *work ethic*; we lay alongside our obsession with work as a key way of achieving status the equally important biblical claim that humans are fulfilled in leisure too. We already see the consequences of the leisure explosion as the working week is reduced and holidays increase. We have not begun to dream of what might be when the high-tech revolution really hits that mass of routine work which can now be automated so cheaply. Much greater upheavals still lie ahead.

No theological exploration which fails to earth itself in practical activity can be said to be Christian and incarnational. But prayerful and worshipful exploration of God's world and his will for it always leads us into caring, costly and risky action.

For most of us, until recently, *work* was paid, contractual employment lasting about forty hours a week for an undisturbed lifetime. Now a somewhat more complicated view is forced upon us. It is still 'paid and contractual' for some, but fewer, people; it is dole-regarded for others who might be seen as having withdrawn from the demand for scarce paid work so that others can have it; it is still institutionalized overtime for surprisingly large proportions of our population; it is moonlighting or black economy or fiddling for employed and unemployed alike; it is home-based activity in DIY and family building; it is volountary 'work' done of free choice, for love and now actively encouraged by goverment in return for expenses, if unemployed; it is that expanding activity we call education, training and retraining which, with effort, equips us for all the above expressions of 'work'; it is political activity (paid and voluntary) which creates the forum out of which new patterns can emerge; and recreation has also become a growing industry, while also remaining a voluntary area in which we freely choose to take part and can find great fulfilment.

What a confusion work is today! God's call to us in this century is to force this confusion out into the open and face it squarely; to minimize the agonies and injustices inherent in change and sadly concentrated in regions like ours; to work towards new and more satisfying patterns of work which engage the full range of skills, talents and energies that God has given to us all; and, remembering the nature of Christ's church, to take a world-embracing view of the future. The North East is not the only place where radically disturbing things are happening to work!

9 Signs of the Kingdom in Sunderland: Fair Trade Shop at Bishopwearmouth

JUDITH WARD · BETTY EAST
MARY DUNCAN · BERNARD DUNCAN

As Christians we frequently pray 'Hallowed be thy name, thy kingdom come, thy will be done on earth . . .' What is the implication of this prayer? What is the kingdom we pray for? It is not an earthly kingdom in this world's sense, a kingdom of might and power, with some lording it over others, as Jesus himself told us (Matt. 20.25). It is a kingdom of justice and of peace, to be established most certainly among men and women on earth, not just a kingdom to be experienced 'in heaven': 'on earth as in heaven'. We do not pray 'may we come to thy kingdom where thy will is done'. We pray for the establishment of justice and peace on earth, as part of the just God's just plan. And if we pray for it, we must 'take up the cross', follow Jesus' way, and live and work for it.

Jesus became incarnate, became flesh, in order to show in his life the kingdom of God at work – to restore the kingdom which is clearly seen as existing in the beginning (Genesis), when man and God were at one, 'walking together'. Jesus proclaimed himself to be the Way, the Truth, the Life. Simply, as Peter said, he 'was filled with the power of the Holy Spirit and went about doing good' (Acts 10.38). When asked if he was the one who was promised, he merely pointed to his work, his ministry. He showed, in other words, by his deeds that he was what his name says, Jesus, 'Jahweh saves'. Jesus was restoring the justice of

41

creation, the kingdom of God, and opposing all that was not just, that was an inversion of the true order, and especially the affliction and oppression imposed by powerful men.

In so doing, Jesus inevitably ran up against the powers of this world, including the powers of his own religion and its laws and practices: 'The kingdom of God is not a matter of what you eat or what you drink, but of justice and peace and the joy that is given by the Holy Spirit of God' (Rom. 14.17). He threw down the challenge: 'Unless your justice exceeds that of the scribes and Pharisees, you shall not be in the kingdom' (Matt. 5.20). Preaching a kingdom different from the norms of the world, Jesus found himself in confrontation with the institutional forms of his day, religious, political, social and economic. As a consequence, the leaders of the institutions conspired to eliminate him, with an excuse that sounds all too familiar: 'for the good of the nation', as John says (11.50).

For nation, substitute national security, shareholders' interest, etc. In the end, Jesus was removed for subversion, to use the term applied in South Africa against Allan Boesak among many. Reflecting on all of this, in his priestly prayer, to his Father, on the evening before his death, Jesus declared that the world did not know the Father, but that he knew him because he was himself the true reflection of God's justice. Those around him now were capable of knowing the Father because Jesus had revealed his name to them – as revealed in the whole process of creation and liberation (Jer. 23.1) – and his name is Justice. And the great prayer which he gave to them begins, in addressing our Father, 'Hallowed be thy name, thy kingdom come, thy will be done on earth'.

This is what is behind our association with Traidcraft through a small shop in the centre of Sunderland. Traidcraft is a Christian organization, with a basis of faith that recognizes the connection between Christ's own life and work and the need for justice and peace in today's society. To quote from one of Traidcraft's own leaflets:

People who belong to Jesus Christ and so enter into the joy of salvation are called to a life of thankfulness, service and stewardship in the whole of their lives and beings. This commits Christians to the costly love of their neighbours, especially when they are the victims of poverty, disease, discrimination, distress and oppression. Christians work for justice and love in the world in response to God's own commitment and character as one who is just and loving.

One of the great sources of institutional oppression in our days is trade. Traidcraft confronts the institutions of trade and all their injustices – exploitation of poor and powerless people's labour, land and commodities – and provides an alternative to them. It rewards labour justly, it helps the people keep their land, it encourages them to develop and use their own commodities and skills, it acts as their link, in a just way, with the rest of the world, including very much ourselves, in the North East and elsewhere in Britain, who act as the links and are ourselves often exploited by the institutions of trade, and perhaps unwittingly take part in the exploiting.

Traidcraft is a partnership for change. The thousands of producers of goods in the Third World are linked with thousands of consumers in this country through the items sold. Fair wages are paid to the producers; fair prices are charged to the consumers. What is absent is vast profits to middlemen, high-powered advertising, costly overheads, exploitation of the powerless. We believe that we are part of a just system of trade with partners overseas. That is why we support Traidcraft.

We had acted individually as representatives of Traidcraft for some time. In 1983 space became available in Bishopwearmouth Church, and as a joint venture the Fair Trade Shop had its beginning. An ecumenical committee was set up to oversee the running of the shop, and volunteers were sought to staff the shop. Posters, newspaper articles and leaflets to the clergy were part of the initial publicity. The shop carries not only a whole range of Third World crafts, but wholefoods, re-cycled paper, and books and pamphlets on development, the environment and related issues.

Our successes have been in the volume of sales, £5,000 in the first year, and in being invited to events around the area to sell and to talk about the products on sale. The end of the first year brought more publicity.

Against this we must set various disappointments. Not many churches have supplied volunteers for the shop. Most helpers come from just two committed churches. The clergy have not been in the forefront in responding to the shop's requests for helpers, or drawing attention to the existence and purpose of the shop.

Sadly too, our educational materials do not bring much response. We had hoped to encourage more thoughtful buying, but self interest still dominates. However, we hope that the shop will continue to be a witness to our 'hunger and thirst for justice' in the months and years ahead, and in being linked with representatives and consumers throughout the country, and with Traidcraft itself, with its remarkable development over seven years and its new links with CAFOD and Christian Aid, we may be one link in the catalyst for change and challenge to the institutions.

Traidcraft, the source of the Fair Trade Shop, is a sign (or sacrament) of the possibility of justice and true partnership in trade and relationships between people and between nations. It is a sign of the kingdom.

10 | *The Hermitage, Shepherd's Law*

JOHN LOWEN

> When I was shown the hovel where O'Neill lived and the oratory where he spent hours in prayer, I could not help feeling that it was a more important place in the history of India than many a battlefield marked by crossed swords upon a map.

These words of Father Benson's come vividly to mind every time I recall my first visit to Shepherd's Law and Brother Harold. There on a hill top in a little hermitage set appropriately amidst the ruins of a 'folly', I could not help feeling that I was in the presence of something as important and significant for the 'kingdom of God' as all the busy schemes and strategies that I was currently involved in or knew of. Indeed, I wondered whether such schemes and strategies could ever be of lasting significance or come to fruition unless supported and informed by something like Shepherd's Law and someone like Br Harold. The 'truisms' about prayer and the Christian's vocation to offer this world and his life and activity to God, that had 'rattled around in the dry and empty garret' of my mind, somehow shifted to my 'heart' and became living 'truths', as I glimpsed something of the contemplative's calling to hold the needs of this poor, dear, broken, frightened yet redeemed world before God. Some Christians, I know, associate the contemplative life with 'escaping from' or 'denying' the 'real' world and view it as being a bit unhealthy and introspective. I had never thought like this but I was unprepared for the difference I found between the Christian way of life I knew and tried to live by, and the way of life on Shepherd's Law. It was quieter, more silent, based more upon a watching and a waiting upon God: and yet it was not inactive. It was a life that breathed God in, and I sensed that Shepherd's Law stood in the same relationship to busy Christian congregations as lungs to an active body. The harder Christians around him laboured the more deeply Br Harold and the life of Shepherd's Law breathed in. I discovered that my concerns and the concerns of the wider church were Br Harold's concerns – but we reacted in different ways. He was concerned to breathe in, to oxygenate the blood, so that the limbs might keep moving and the brain remain clear and active.

At first, along with being puzzled, I think I was a trifle arrogant and more than a little piqued – somewhat like Naaman the Syrian when Elisha told him to bathe in the Jordan – 'are not . . . the rivers of Damascus better than all the waters of Israel? Can I not wash in them and be clean?' 'Are there not churches throughout the land?' I thought, 'Can we not pray in them? Cannot we active Christians make room for stillness and silence, and inform our own activity with reflective prayer?' But I knew only too well, as the vicar of a busy and active suburban parish, how easy it was for myself and others to forget God in the midst of well-meaning activity (indeed even to forget the meaning of the activity itself); and I recalled that it is hard to teach yourself what you do not know. In short, I felt that we active, busy Christians needed to be prayed for, as much as we ourselves needed to pray; that we needed to be taught, as much as we needed to teach; and that it was unlikely that our activity would succeed unless we were reminded what it was for. I began to think that the contemplative calling was not just an interesting feature of the 'Body of Christ', to cover up or adorn according to taste, but, perhaps, a vital and necessary, life-giving organ. With thoughts such as these moving from my mind to my heart, I left Shepherd's Law.

Over the following year or so, I kept in touch with Br Harold, and he spoke of his sense of communion with the saints of Northumbria – of the fact that monks played a large part in a bygone 'dark' age to keep alive learning, worship and the faith. He spoke of a sense in which a new darkness may be rising in the hearts of men, and a new breed of lost, restless questing barbarians emerging. And finally he spoke of his hope of establishing, with God's grace, a little contemplative community at Shepherd's Law. To raise in a sense a 'watch-tower', to set a beacon on a hill both as a warning and as a 'light to lighten the gentiles'. To establish a place of sanctuary for the broken and wounded to find healing and peace, a place that would inform our activity and witness to the mystery, beauty, strangeness and humility of the kingdom of God. I invited him to come and talk to a prayer group and our Parochial Church Council about his way of life, and he came and asked them for help.

The request took us by surprise, and we were not at all sure what to say. Ours is a numerous, busy, active, middle-class suburban seaside parish, and although we had encountered many things, we had never before met someone who had built with his bare hands a hermitage in order to live on a hill top and pray. Amongst us we had people who understood business and finance, who thought a lot about society and its needs, who acknowledged that it was the duty of Christians to worship God. But we were unused to silence, contemplative prayer and hermits, and Br Harold came upon us like something out of a sketch by John Cleese. Feelings of puzzlement, embarrassment and curiosity were evident. We wondered whether such a venture was either practicable or even desirable in this day and age. To some it sounded simply odd and foolish. To others the risks attached to it were too great: where would the other members of such a community come from? Would anyone come, or would we be left with a rebuilt folly? Would Br Harold die and the Franciscans and other orders find the building useless? Could the building even be built, could it be heated, would anyone see any point to it, even if it could be done? Could anything good come from Nazareth? The questions went on and on, and to many there were, and still are, no answers.

It was strange though that all who were engaged in researching this project found themselves continually faced by the question: 'What do you really believe about me? Do you believe anything at all?' We were faced continually with the mystery of the Trinity and our own pride and frailty. Eventually, a year ago, we unanimously decided to help with the project. We remembered that our God is a God of surprises, who uses unlikely, hidden, humble or foolish things to forward his kingdom, and with a good deal of heart-searching we decided to build. Things have gone reasonably well to date, but I must confess that we worry continually whether our approach witnesses to 'the folly of God' wherein there is wisdom, or merely to our own stupidity. We worry too that in the building of Shepherd's Law we will bury what we found there. But we busy Christians are prone to anxiety, and the silence we seek to enshrine there soothes us, and the light we seek to place there guides us.

Our aims for Shepherd's Law are sevenfold:

1. To state openly that the summit of the church's vocation is the worship of God, and that the true end of humanity is the vision of God.

2. To witness to the priority of God in the life of men and women, and to the need for conversion of the heart.

3. To witness to the communion of saints and the need of the church for reconciliation and unity in one diverse fellowship.

4. To bear witness to the faith that has been handed down to us, so that the present generation may be faithful in its stewardship of what has been received and reflect how best it can be adapted to the needs of the future.

5. To keep alive the prophetic tradition in our Judaeo-Christian heritage. The ones who are moulded by and come from the 'wilderness' have much to say.

6. To provide a place of silence, stillness and solitude where men and women may open their hearts to God and learn a little more about him and themselves, and hopefully grow a little in the image of his Son.

7. To provide a place where the common life is a 'school of charity' in which conversion may be deepened and love grow, a place where 'young men may see visions and old men dream dreams'.

11 | St Peter's Enterprises Ltd YTS Training Workshop

STEPHEN PEDLEY

St Peter's, Stockton, dates as a parish from 1875, and since 1978 has belonged with three other parishes in what is called the Central Stockton Anglican Group of Parishes. Both parochial and sector ministers belong to the group. Sector ministers are clergy who exercise specialist ministries, for instance, in industrial mission, education, hospital chaplaincies. One of the group's main objects has been the real and visible complementarity of the parochial and sector ministries. Until recently one of the sector ministers was the Community Chaplain and his ministry was chiefly exercised amongst the people and groups and institutions within the town which the churches hardly touched. It was largely through his ministry, through visits to our Parochial Church Council (PCC), and through sermons and discussions, that St Peter's became really conscious of the growing problem of youth unemployment in Stockton and in Cleveland.

Meanwhile, St Peter's was only too aware of its under-used and dilapidated hall. Through a conscious decision (and as a result of much fund raising) another building in another part of the parish was renovated for parish use to allow the old hall 'to be given away'. The decision was not unanimous and the surrender caused quite a lot of pain in some quarters. A scheme to use it as a community centre with the help of the local Council failed. At the end of a general parish meeting about individual and corporate responses to unemployment the Community Chaplain suggested that the hall might be used for an MSC Youth Training Scheme with the PCC as sponsor. A Mode B Scheme was suggested by which there would be fifty places for trainees to come to the hall for a year to develop skills like pottery and woodwork. A feasibility study was undertaken, the idea was accepted, and an agreement was entered, money was spent to make the hall good, and in November 1982 the Directors of St Peter's Enterprises Ltd (all laypeople from St Peter's congregation) appointed the manager.

From that appointment all else has flowed: the re-ordering of the hall to accommodate the scheme and the appointment of the necessary staff (the parish providing ten per cent of all capital expenditure); and the further development of the hall to make room for a Mode A Scheme which opened in 1984 involving a further one hundred trainees and yet more staff (now fourteen). A Mode A Scheme manages trainees in job placements for a year in the community and brings them back to base in phases for further training. Now, in line with what we believe to be government policy, the Mode B Scheme and the Mode A Scheme have been merged and the year's term extended to two years.

Now the advocates for the scheme have had to think out a pastoral and theological and practical justification for it in the thick of some pretty articulate opposition both at Annual Meetings and Church Councils. It has not been an easy ride though the scheme has made St Peter's, Stockton, far better known, in particular in the secular community, locally and nationally. It is interesting that a lot of support has come from the immediate neighbourhood of the hall (what one might describe as a working class neighbourhood) where people claim they see the parish involving itself in 'real issues' for a change.

We believe that the church as a sacrament of God's presence with his people must be a sign of his kingdom in the midst of the community – not simply a sign of love and care but also a sign of justice and peace. Regardless of our success or failure with our trainees, and regardless of the element of risk involved (we do not know where it will all end and sometimes some things seem to be beyond our control), we believe it is vital for us 'to be present' with them and to identify ourselves with their needs. A lot of this identification results in quite ordinary pastoral and practical

50

contact but a lot of it also involves management and that involves us in a lot of real issues like staff structures, wages, dismissals, etc. We proclaim that all that must be within the kingdom.

We believe that presence leads on to reconciliation. We not only give but we also receive. Because of inevitable contacts between trainees and parishioners (some of the plant is in fact shared by both parties), there has been reconciliation of a sort across the generations and both camps begin to see each other with a human face and friendships are made.

We believe that nothing is possible without sacrifice and surrender. The daily celebration of the eucharist must bear visible fruit. Dying to something held dear opens up new possibilities for life. This is not only realized within the life of the workshop but in the creation of a whole network of relationships within the town and the community of which we are now a very real member (a new concept of the Body of Christ?). It also makes us seek out new venues for work in our part of the parish. In our part of Stockton there are many different churches, all with extensive plant which we are learning more and more to share.

We believe that our immediate practical response, in so far as it is truly Christian in motivation, has lasting and eternal value and worth. Amongst a group of directors, some of whom are very professional businessmen, there are sometimes ambivalances here. What is good Christianity may not be good business nor good management. Or is it? We simply offer all that we do, and all the opportunities that hopefully it opens to God for him to use. And in so doing we receive back from many different quarters a lot of fun, enjoyment and fulfilment.

12 | Minsteracres Monastery Projects

ANDREW O'CONNOR · LUKE MAGEE

The Congregation of the Passion (normally known as Passionists) established a foundation at Minsteracres in 1950. Our Rule states:

> We seek the unity of our lives and our apostolate in the Passion of Jesus. Because we are aware that his Passion continues in this world until he comes in glory, we share in the joys and struggles of people in their journey to the Father.

In 1975 Passionists in England and Wales met to examine their lives and work according to the principles of 'prospective planning' established by the Christian industrialist, Gaston Berger. One of the objectives then formulated was: 'To create a gospel community which is a dynamic presence of love and concern whose members are engaged in constant dialogue with the world and involved in its joys and sufferings.' This was to lead us at Minsteracres to ask not only how we were forming the community which surrounded us but also how it was forming us. We wanted to make a preferential option for the poor, especially in our area for those who were being marginalized and excluded from significant participation in the mainstream culture and activity of society, for people who had either lost a role in life or had never been able to find one. This is not really an option for the Christian because it is God's option. Jesus defined his mission in Luke 4.18: 'he has sent me to bring the good news to the poor, to proclaim liberty to captives and to the blind new sight, to set the downtrodden free'. Matthew (ch. 25) tells us that one day we shall be faced with our response to real poverty. It is not so much what we can do for the poor as what being with them may do for us. God has always made the poor part of the revelation of his kingdom and has spoken very powerfully through them. God is at his best in the poverty and weakness of Calvary.

Something of the vision was clearly stated by Pope Paul VI in his 'Apostolic Exhortation on the Renewal of Religious Life':

> How then will the cry of the poor find an echo in your lives? That cry must, first of all, bar you from whatever would be a compromise with any form of social injustice. It obliges you also to awaken consciences to the drama of misery and to the demands of social justice made by the gospel and the church. It leads some of you to join the poor in their situation and to share their bitter cares.

We saw the clouds of unemployment already gathering over Consett. The closing of British Steel was soon to take place, putting 4,000 people out of work. We began to examine our resources and the ways in which we could help. Discussions were already in progress with Andrew O'Connor who was asking how he could give the last ten years of his working life to the church and the community. He became the first director of our projects.

We decided to proceed on two levels:

1. To alleviate the consequences of unemployment by establishing practical projects for those without paid work.

2. (*a*) To enable groups of unemployed and those affected by unemployment to examine the general and specific consequences of unemployment in their lives and to enable them to develop alternative strategies to cope with those consequences.

(*b*) To establish liaison with groups and individuals and service departments concerned with the unemployed.

For the past nine years we have been working together to alleviate wherever possible the problem of unemployment in the local community. Eight of the nine years have been in active involvement on schemes we have sponsored and which have grown from our initial intake of 12 persons in July 1977 to 320 places in 1985, and during this period we have found temporary employment for a total of 1,422 persons. Yet this is but a tiny fraction of the 'non-working' populace of over 220,859 in the Northern Counties of which there are some 26,500 young persons in the diocese of Hexham and Newcastle.

The initial scheme was mounted in July 1977 under the then Job Creation Programme which permitted adult and youth groups to work together. There were sixteen persons in the group, and the project was the refurbishment of disused huts which had been sleeping quarters for the National Fire Service, and their conversion into a residential youth centre to house up to thirty-four persons. This project was completed in July 1978.

During this time a start was made on a second project, the conversion of the fire engine garages as a potential Training Workshop. This scheme was then extended to include a gardening project. Greenhouses, potting sheds and general housing were renovated in the kitchen garden, an area of one and a half acres.

Involvement with the horticultural aspect brought into focus the situation in the surrounding woodlands, and additional recruitment of unemployed people resulted in the start of a third scheme under a trained forester.

In addition to the above project we were able to offer work to people in the arts and special skills area. A number of unemployed fine art restorers were recruited under the STEP scheme (Special Temporary Employment Project). These have restored the ornamental ceilings, the tapestries and walls in the original ballroom of the Community house. This was a highly specialized undertaking and gave employment to the group for fourteen months.

During the period 1978/79 the schemes were developed and consolidated. The Training Workshop was fitted out with machinery and a start was made on the production of rustic furniture and also requirements for the building section.

One building in the garden area was set aside as a metal workshop and work put in hand to equip it. The orchard was replanted (the existing trees being badly cankered). A tree nursery was planted with a total of 5,000 trees for various areas in the woodland. The Forestry came into full operation; thinning and brashing out work was undertaken as well as a programme of drainage, site clearance and other arboricultural activities including the supply of prepared timber for the woodwork section of the Training Workshop.

55

A supply of electricity was put into the garden by underground cable. It was carried out by young people under skilled supervision at a cost of £700 – 37% of the North of England Electricity Board's estimate.

Towards the end of 1979 the scope of the schemes was extended to involve the wider community, and approval was given by the MSC to sponsor a PBWE (Project Based Work Experience) scheme at sites in the Durham area.

There were now five schemes in operation and with unemployment still increasing a feasibility study into further commitment was commenced. During the period 1979/80 the staffing of the schemes totalled one hundred and three.

A joint decision relating to scheme formation was reached with the MSC in late 1980. The existing schemes were to be restructured under new agreements, to give greater flexibility in both financial and administrative procedures. We were also urged to increase the number of personnel, if possible, to two hundred places. The new agreements began in April 1981.

An in-depth study of facilities for the disabled was undertaken, and as a result we started a gardening and woodworking scheme for the disabled at St Joseph's Mission, Burn Hall, Durham, the home of the Mill Hill Fathers, who generously put buildings and land at our disposal. As a result of its success a similar scheme was mounted at Minsteracres and is proving of great benefit.

A derelict council depot building was converted and now serves as a Resource Centre for a local community, giving facilities for woodwork, metal work, vehicle repair, arts and crafts, photography, etc. It also serves as headquarters for a Community Care Group dealing with the aged and infirm, including gardening and decorating.

An adult literacy scheme under our Voluntary Projects Programme is also based in the Centre.

13

Hearing Voices: A Changing Curriculum for a Changing Society

RICHARD NICHOLSON

If, for a moment, we personify the secondary school, we can see she is suffering role-conflict as never before. If she is a listening school, there are many voices competing for her ear, some whispering insidiously, some shouting fairly raucously. In this veritable babel, how does the listening school decide its curriculum? The need is to find a dynamic which will enable everyone (pupils, parents, teachers, community) to articulate their needs, not in a shouting match but in a working relationship. We must avoid a dialogue of the deaf.

Listening to teachers

Let us begin with the teachers. The almost feudal power structures still operating in many secondary schools are inimical to creative change. Rigid line management, however benign the individuals in the line, tends to lead to inertia, since everyone is waiting for someone else to take initiatives. Where teachers are encouraged to express themselves, whatever their position in the hierarchy, and to work in overlapping teams towards common objectives, agreed by consensus, they will create their own dynamic for change. This implies a radical change in the politics of the school, challenging the traditional role of the headteacher as the one who holds most of the levers of power, and challenging the Head of Department Barons who tend to build and defend their own territorial empires, even if they have no further territorial demands. We at Sheraton Grange School (Cleveland) evolved decision-making and power-sharing systems which involved, in turn, every member of the teaching and non-teaching staff who wanted to be involved, and pupils, working together. One of our best committees is the capitation committee. This headteacher has lost that power of partronage!

The best model we evolved for curriculum development was the problem-solving working party, which, again, tapped the energy and ideas of all staff, irrespective of their positions in the hierarchy – there are too few occasions when Scale 1 teachers can work creatively with more experienced colleagues. School-based curriculum development offers staff development opportunities – opportunities for refreshment, renewal, and growth – in a dramatically altered job opportunity scene for teachers. We set up such a group to review the school's existing arrangements for personal development education and social education across the curriculum, and to make recommendations (in organizational terms, curricular terms, and in terms of methodology) with a view to achieving greater integration and coherence in the social education to be provided in future. After drawing in contributions from colleagues in all subject areas they came up with an overall conceptual framework to be used with all years in a compulsory core programme called SPD (Social and Personal Development).

In this working party teachers indicated their own in-service needs which were then met, in the main, by their own colleagues in this collaborative mode of learning. We had a practical work-shop on games and devices for ice-breaking in group work and did a lot together to improve our understanding of the group dynamic and the skills needed to 'chair' group discussion. Teachers need to know that all groups work through the stages of forming, storming, norming, and performing (otherwise they will be very worried when they encounter difficulties in the early stages). They have to learn to tolerate silence and develop other skills needed to discourage dependency on the teacher as a group leader.

Listening to pupils

Then we must listen to the pupils. If we open our ears to how they articulate their needs they may well begin by talking in terms of 'O' levels to get jobs (we have probably conditioned them well). But if we engage them in a proper dialogue, again in a working relationship, they soon move beyond this superficial response. Our recent experience has confirmed my view that pupils are ready and able to take a number of creative roles, in decision-making, curriculum planning, curriculum evaluation, self-evaluation, and assessment.

We invited pupils to attend the team meetings where we planned our social and personal development lessons. There were teething troubles (a lot of learning even there), but pupils proved their ability not only to suggest curriculum content but to offer ideas on methodology and suggest strategies for helping disaffected pupils become more involved and better motivated. Negotiated curriculum gives pupils a stake in what goes on, so outcomes are likely to be more successful, and the process itself is a potent vehicle for learning. Planning how to make work interesting and meaningful to their peers is not a problem-solving exercise, it is real!

Once the broad curriculum framework had been jointly planned, groups were able to plan their own approaches in detail. If a group wants to visit leisure centres and other places of recreation, they do the telephoning and make all the arrangements. One pupil experience of taking responsibility is worth hundreds of words of exhortation from teachers about the desirability of developing a sense of responsibility. In some schools pupils are kept in a state of dependency until they arrive in fifth year where their teachers bemoan their inability to show initiative.

When the whole fourth year went out of school to learn from the workplace, they kept a diary and evaluated the experience and their responses. Because work experience was part of a course, these fourth years had been prepared for some of the challenges; they had some say in where they were placed; they had been interviewed by the employers beforehand; and they were given support by teachers visiting regularly once they started. They had real-life experiences rather than vicarious ones. They were expected to reflect on the experience at the time and when they returned to school – a useful teaching/learning model. The final write-up included their own evaluation and the teacher's, and became part of their school record of achievement – a useful model of assessment.

Listening to the community

Again, the needs of the community should not be communicated from long-range but in face-to-face encounters in working relationships. If the school is to 'belong' to the community in a sense which implies much more than access through the doors, community involvement must penetrate the curriculum. In some parts of the country adults other than teachers are getting into schools, but most are professional and middle-class and they are working mainly in social education and careers programmes leaving other areas of the curriculum practically unaffected. Adults other than teachers can and should participate in curriculum reappraisal and curriculum development as well as in implementing teaching programmes. One of the most creative members of the working party which reappraised our curriculum before we set up our social and personal development programme was an industrial chaplain. Craft Design Technology, for instance, is an area of the curriculum where adults other than teachers could make a valuable contribution, particularly considering the number of talented people available because of redundancy, early retirement, and unemployment.

The community is an important educational resource and we must help young people seek out and use to the full all the employment, occupational, educational, and recreational opportunities in their environment. At the same time pupils can help develop the community while at school and as future community members. The community should help shape the school and the school should be a change agent in the community. If these arguments appear to lead us in circles that is exactly as it should be.

It is not my intention here to advocate a particular curriculum, since that would contradict my thesis that the curriculum should emerge from discussion between all interested parties as a response to their particular needs in their peculiar situations. I have, rather, offered a model for creating a dynamic for change in the curriculum. I will, however, venture to suggest that some elements should be common core and no pupil should be denied access by reason of gender, age, ability, or the idiosyncrasies of timetabling. These elements (and I am thinking of all ages and abilities) include study skills, experiential learning, learning from the group dynamic, learning from the workplace, negotiated curriculum and contract learning, community education, political education, health and sex education, and learning about child development and parenting. People talk a lot about the basics; what could be more basic than this list? If the way we organize in secondary schools cuts some pupils off from these areas we may have to rethink the recent orthodoxy about compulsory and optional elements of the curriculum.

Listening to parents

I have not said much about parents specifically, partly because I see parents as auxiliary teachers who can get involved in the curriculum. They need not merely stand on the sidelines shouting encouragement, as it were, through fund-raising and other traditional PTA activities – important though fund-raising is these days. PTAs must include educational events that encourage real participation, as well as the other events. Parent Governors should get into the schools and join in working groups with all the others I have mentioned.

Given the unpredictable nature of the future, apart from the near certainty of accelerating change, qualities like adaptability, self-reliance, and the acceptance of responsibility are likely to serve society's needs best, and these qualities are encouraged by interactive modes of learning where people encounter people.

14 | Brunswick Methodist Church Newcastle Upon Tyne

DAVID DRIVER

Brunswick Methodist Church in the heart of Newcastle upon Tyne is today very much a city centre church situated as it is in the midst of an extremely busy shopping area. It has not always been so central. When the church was opened in 1821 it lay on the northern fringes of the city and catered for a largely residential population. From the outset it was well attended, a key Methodist Church on Tyneside, whose membership included numbers of the leading figures and families in nineteenth-century Newcastle.

It is helpful to paint in this background because Brunswick's situation now is vastly different and an understanding of its present opportunities has to bear this in mind. No longer is there a sizeable residential community anywhere near and while more living accommodation is being provided in the city centre it is mainly for singles or couples but rarely families. Meanwhile the commercial heart of the city has moved up the hill from near the Tyne and Brunswick now stands amidst a regional shopping complex drawing its customers from a huge area. From Monday to Saturday the daytime streets around are always busy and at the high seasons they are overloaded with people. In the evenings and on Sundays it is much quieter.

The question which Brunswick has had to face is how to minister to circumstances so very different from its earlier life. What witness to the kingdom of God can it offer to the transient crowds

63

which throng the midweek thoroughfares? Where, in this context, is the judgment and mercy, the hope and healing of the Lord, to which it must be a sign?

It has to be remembered that Brunswick is only one of a number of city centre churches linked together through a central Council of Churches. No one congregation can bear the whole weight of witness, and must never delude itself that it could, and certainly not to the rich kaleidoscope of a city centre. We are glad, for example, that the United City Centre Chaplaincy ministers to many in the business and commercial communities, spheres with which Brunswick has only general contact.

The work of the kingdom is wider than any one congregation can encompass but that still leaves in question the witness of each church. The vision that came to the people of Brunswick when faced with this query a few years ago was that they should transform their old and venerable buildings. The result has been a complex of premises, with a worshipping centre at its heart, that enables a wide variety of welcoming, caring and training activities to flourish. And flourish they do. The church is open seven days a week and certainly from Monday to Saturday it has never been so busy in its existence.

The focal point of our transformed building is the worshipping centre because worship is for us, as for every other church, the heart of our life. Whatever the changes in the city centre it is vital for its health that God's name should be praised there. That lies at the core of all our witness so that worship is both basis and climax of all that we do. Moreover, we still have a sizeable congregation, particularly on Sunday evenings, which needs to be nourished and inspired. Preaching has always been a distinctive mark of Brunswick's life. It still is. City centre congregations attract visitors, strangers, students, passers by as well as being arenas for various special services. The proclamation of the gospel is one of the marks of the kingdom of God and we believe it is a calling to which we must give high priority.

In planning our renewed premises we decided to create a Sandwich Bar in the entrance area which would open each midweek lunchtime and would add to the Saturday morning and afternoon refreshments that had long been provided. It was intended to be a service of welcome, a simple act of hospitality provided by our church people. From the outset the numbers

64

who have come day by day have amazed us. It is a service which has engendered much good will. We do not pretend that it is profound ministry but it does open doors to deeper conversations and to other areas of church life. These bridges to and from the Christian family to the community around are very important. They may become avenues into the kingdom of God.

In fact we view the whole use of our buildings along these lines. We have attractive and versatile premises strategically placed for many gatherings. We encourage their use both by a wide range of Christian organizations and by numerous secular caring and community groups. So, for example, both Alcoholics Anonymous and Gamblers Anonymous meet here every week, and they are two of very many bodies which congregate here over the course of a year. It is our express policy to use the premises as a centre of witness and a house of care.

There are two distinctive ministries which have been pioneered in response to city centre needs. One is our Youth Project where we employ two full time youth workers. Its aim is to relate to the young people who frequent the heart of the city. Some work there, some are truanting, and others, for whom we feel particular concern, are unemployed. We run a separate coffee bar for young people each midweek lunchtime and certain teatimes as well. In addition to their work on the premises both workers go out on the streets meeting and befriending young people where they gather.

Our two youth workers now have access to a youth world and culture right beyond the life of any church. They are themselves bridges between the two realms. The friendships they have made have enabled a prodigious amount of help to be sought and given on matters ranging from accommodation to pregnancies, glue sniffing to family deaths and breakdowns. There have been outings together, days away, and at times deep discussions about the meaning of life. Links have been formed with the life of the church and in any case the Youth Project enables young people from the church and others with no religious affiliation whatsoever to mingle together. We see these efforts as an outworking of God's unconditional love for people in this neighbourhood. It is an offer of friendship and acceptance to young people, many of whom feel alienated and unvalued, just as and where they are.

The Youth Project is also involved in building bridges between separate and sometimes hostile groups of young people. For example, after long contacts on the streets a group of skinheads at last started coming to the coffee bar. Some of them were involved with the National Front which soon sent some of its local leaders to investigate the company their members were keeping. They did not approve of our coffee bar with its reconciling, accepting approach and with its avowed Christian basis which is neither forced nor kept hidden. Happily the work with the skinheads continues very actively. And the links grow; one skinhead mother has just started bringing her little boy to Sunday School.

The young people the Youth Project is relating to are very largely those rejected by their families, schools, and society in general. We see it as Christ's calling to stand alongside them. In addition, we try where possible to readdress the labels which society places all too easily on such people, and also where possible to challenge the structures which create the injustices and inequalities which we frequently find here. This, too, we believe, is part of the necessary witness to the kingdom of God.

The other distinctive ministry to those around is Listening Post. Jesus spoke about those in the crowds of his own day who were 'harassed and helpless'. Listening Post exists for their counterparts today. Numerous statutory and voluntary bodies care for such people of course and the last thing we wish to do is to duplicate their work. But we became convinced at Brunswick that a deep area of need still persists. Most agencies, however caring, simply do not have time to listen extensively to their clients and in today's frequently lonely society there are many who feel that they have no one to whom they can unburden themselves. Yet the burdens are there and they can be crushing. So, a dozen years ago, Listening Post was opened. It has its own small suite of rooms and a team of trained listeners who offer a welcome to everyone who calls and to whom anyone in whatever sort of need can speak freely and in confidence. Listening Post is open six afternoons and three evenings a week.

From the outset Listening Post has been ecumenical, drawing on the gifts of Christians from all sections of the church in the service of troubled folk. It has its own Director, an Advisory Council of people with a variety of professional skills, and a current team of about fifty listeners. The listeners are drawn from many walks of life and have all undergone a careful training and selection process. We believe that the quality of attentive and understanding listening should be of a high level, and it is worthy of note that Listening Post is both able to call on and to release the skills and kindnesses of ordinary people to make this service possible. It is an agency of the body of Christ and not of a specialist corps within it.

There can be little doubt that a needed service is being provided. Over two thousand visits a year are currently being paid to Listening Post. The range of problems is very wide and sometimes exceptionally deep. We do our best to ensure that people who come to us feel that we have ample time for them and that they are receiving our full attention as persons. We are not an advice bureau nor a counselling agency. What we offer is attentive listening and with it the time and the opportunity for people to express what they feel. That act of unburdening oneself to a discerning friend can be such a release that it is a therapy in itself as well as opening the way to fresh insight and new hope.

Sometimes that fresh insight leads into the spiritual realm. This is a sphere which we do not force but in which as Christian people we are glad to share. It is our conviction that there is a wholeness of body, mind and spirit to which God calls us and it is the joy of Listening Post to see particular men and women being sustained in the midst of trouble and emerging, sometimes quite splendidly, into a new stability and fullness.

Brunswick's position and consequently the form of its ministry has changed considerably over the years. We feel it a privilege to be situated where we are now and to be able to share in God's continuing work of renewing love amidst the teeming life of a city centre.

15 | *Millfield St Mark's Community Project*

PETER ATKINSON

St Mark's Church serves a small, predominantly working class area close to the centre of Sunderland. The population has a considerable percentage of unemployment, a very large proportion of elderly people living alone and a growing number of children. Apart from a school, playgroups and an Over-60s club there are very few community facilities. There is also little space in which children can play.

The project has grown out of an awareness of these social needs of the area, plus the fact that the church possesses a large but delapidated hall which it very rarely uses. This has been a problem for the church for many years. It seemed sensible, therefore, to see if it might be possible to turn what was a burden for the church into something which might be of benefit to the whole community. A steering committee was established comprising community and church representatives which successfully applied for £75,000 for the project through the Urban Aid Programme.

The intention is to convert the church hall into a centre for the neighbourhood in which a number of activities can be housed. Provision will be made, therefore, for sport, an advice centre, a day centre for the elderly, mentally infirm and youth activities. It is also hoped that in some sense it will be an unemployment resource centre. The church will in effect be handing over the building and site to the community, though it will be represented on the management committee, and will thus be initiating a partnership with the community.

Obviously the project has arisen out of a very concrete practicality, that is, what should St Mark's do about a hall in a bad state of repair which it neither uses nor can find the money necessary to put right? There is, however, some theology underpinning the enterprise, at least in the mind of the vicar! It is hoped that the theological concepts will be more widely appreciated and adopted by the congregation as the project develops.

As so often seems to be the case, it is hard to determine which comes first: theology or event. I have always been more world orientated in seeking to respond to the notion of the kingdom, so it is not surprising that I should look to ways of working more closely with the community and its representatives. But the opportunity provided by having to do something about an old church hall has led to the discovery that one or two theological concepts in particular seem relevant and illuminating.

They are, first of all, the basic Old Testament idea of salvation as literally 'the creation of space'. This has an obvious reference to the Promised Land. In the context of the parish of Millfield the community project can be seen as a not dissimilar creation of space – physical, emotional and perhaps potentially spiritual – in which some kind of flourishing can take place against a background of 'oppressions' of one kind or another. The creation of space can also be seen as a response to the liberating consequences of the kingdom as preached by Christ.

The second concept is Christ's 'boundary crossing' ministry. As a motive for mission and as one of the most telling ways in which Christ declared the reversal of values which the kingdom implied, this ministry provides a useful context in which to see the project. It involves a recognition of the fact that the values of the kingdom are furthered by breaking out of the normally accepted ecclesiastical boundaries and categories.

The third concept is the basic Christian belief that it is only by 'letting go' that new opportunities can occur. It is hoped that this exercise in working with a community will help the church to let go of its instinct for survival and self-preservation and discover something new in the process. It could have the effect of persuading the church to take the world seriously as the locus of God's activity.

PART III

The Kingdom of God Today

16 | *The Kingdom of God Today*

The teaching of Jesus makes it clear that the kingdom can and should be expressed in some way on earth. His teaching about it presents us with themes for life and action. We take our cue from him and allow him to show us how to express the kingdom in our contemporary scene.

What we do is, therefore, a response to Jesus' teaching, to Jesus himself, and ultimately to God. This responsive note prevents us from overestimating our *own* performance or achievement. As all good works are prompted by God's Spirit, so ultimately they are God's doing, not ours. We are part of something far greater than ourselves or our world or our times, which has nevertheless found us and given us new vision.

Such statements are theologically conventional: that is how, in general, we understand the kingdom. But there is at least one other aspect of it. To attempt to give expression to the kingdom is to embark on a voyage of adventure. It is to make new discoveries, about God and humankind. It is to be surprised by joy ('fun', says one contributor), and disconcerted by disappointment. It is to act by faith, to take risks and not to have the assurance that one's course is necessarily right or productive. It is to long to see the harvest, and perhaps never to see it. One's perception of the kingdom is sharpened by experience in its service. But this greater awareness of its reality sends us back to Jesus to hear his words again.

In line with this thinking, we must look again at the emphases in each of the above projects: at the experience, the perceptions, the questions and the problems which each raises. It may well be that as they 'perform' the kingdom each in its own way, they in some sense enact new parables of the kingdom for us today: not parables which will supercede the originals, but which will lead us back to them to hear them with fresh understanding.

Take 'Fair Trade' at Bishopwearmouth, for instance. A modest enough procedure, one might think: a few stalls in a church, a small band of helpers, thoughtfully selected third-world wares; just a hint of the 'trendy, Christian left', perhaps, with a gentle seasoning of liberation theology. Is that the picture? Or is there a *parable* here, which brings certain motifs of God's kingdom before our eyes in a fresh way? If so, it is a parable about change. If we say 'thy will be done' in this world, then the structures and the set patterns that bring profit to some and deprivation to others must change. 'Thy will be done' does not admit of cosy domestication and privatization. It does not allow economic systems to escape its challenge. It requires of us to think about how we exploit God's creatures and his creation, and to realize that an account will be required of us. 'The Lord looked for justice . . . and all he found was oppression.' Amos found it hard to discern the working of the kingdom of God in his time except in terms of judgment. The parables of the kingdom can take that kind of turn. Then the going gets really rough. 'Not many churches have supplied volunteers . . . The clergy have not been in the forefront in responding . . .' Echoes of the religious people, clergy and laity, who manage to avoid facing up to the real issues of the kingdom; the Pharisees and Sadducees are not confined to ancient Judaism! 'We had hoped to encourage more thoughtful buying, but self-interest dominates'; we have ears to hear, yet refuse to hear. Yet the work *must* go on, because it is a humble and faithful enactment of the kingdom. The parable of the Sower provides the motif which both informs and sustains (Mark 4.3–8).

Reading through the projects, one cannot but be aware of the great concern, even preoccupation, with the question of employment and unemployment: part-time working, redundancy, early retirement, work-sharing, competition for jobs,

74

training and re-training, the use of leisure – these are only some of the implications. This is the world in which we live, the horizons to so many lives. And with these pressures there arises the urgent need for support, encouragement and understanding, counselling and care; for the strains on individuals, families and communities are immense. These are the motifs of new, contemporary parables which suggest how the kingdom of God may find performance in this harsh world. Sometimes the parable is about enablers who – whether through research, political lobbying or practical schemes – are helping people to come to terms with the problem of employment or unemployment. It is as if one and all were searching for the pearl which is beyond price; or a many-faceted stone which for some involves employment and for some a creative use of an indefinite future without paid work, and for others some kind of mixture of both scenes; but in all cases the answer required is much more than adjusting to the matter of work or no work. It is about fulfilment, peace with self, family and community: ultimately, peace with God. That is the pearl without price, yet it is not attained by any spiritual route which cuts out the pain of adjusting to the realities of life today. The way to find the kingdom, or to be found by it, is through the world of action and inter-action. This is the very stuff of parable.

Sometimes the practical project is itself the parable: 'a lot of support has come from the immediate neighbourhood of the hall . . . where people claim they see the parish involving itself in "real issues" for a change' (Stephen Pedley). The writer (or teller of the parable) moves from the church as a sacrament of God's presence with his people to the church as a sign of the kingdom in the midst of the community. And the sign takes the form of a YTS training workshop, developing practical skills in the context of caring concern and as part of the quest for justice and peace. A parable of the kingdom indeed. The image of the training workshop may be a modern counterpart of the banquet in Jesus' parables, or the table-fellowship in his ministry.

Some of the contributors describe a special effort, such as a campaign to preserve a rural school, with its particular community value and Christian ethos. Others speak of on-going concerns: rural or city evangelism, running a day-centre for the mentally ill, or developing a curriculum that genuinely attempts to meet the needs of the pupils. One cannot fail to identify the emphasis on sensitivity to people as they are, with all their burdens and fears and misgivings. 'Almost all felt rejected by society on account of being mentally ill', Judy Banister writers, 'but gradually we have seen acceptance and tolerance become fellowship and love.' We recall the emphasis in Jesus' ministry on welcoming those whom society has marginalized, and so winning a response from many who found difficulty in responding to any in society. And his characteristic concern for and identification with the vulnerable and defenceless: 'Truly, I say to you, as you did it (not) to one of the least of these my brethren, you did it (not) to me' (Matt. 25.40; cf. 25.45). Richard Nicholson emphasizes the need to *listen* to what people are trying to say – whether teachers, pupils, community or parents . . . 'We must avoid a dialogue of the deaf'. One of the signs of the kingdom is that the deaf hear and the dumb speak. And the servants of the kingdom are those who, through loving actions, enable the deaf to discern a message and the dumb to find their voices again when all was previously silence.

Peter Atkinson invokes the Old Testament notion of salvation as 'the creation of space'. This is, in fact, to use the Exodus story as a kind of parable: the struggle of God's people to find space in which to be themselves. A community project may aim to do precisely this – or at least, to set the process in motion. It involves 'a not dissimilar creation of space, physical, emotional and perhaps potentially spiritual in which some human flourishing can take place against a background of "oppressions" of one kind or another'. One of the intriguing features of the Exodus story as parable of liberation is the negative side implicit in the narrative. Space they needed, and space they eventually achieved – but at the cost of oppressing others (e.g., the peoples of the land).

The Exodus parable remains tremendously evocative – perhaps all the more thought-provoking because of the issues it raises. The complete liberation motif, however, is that of the kingdom of God, in which the creation of space is probably a more basic element than is often allowed. One of the more difficult sayings to interpret is Luke 17.20–21: 'The kingdom of God is not coming with signs to be observed; nor will they say, "Lo here it is!" or "There!" for behold, the kingdom of God is in the midst of you' (RSV). In this saying, Jesus seems to be correcting an exaggerated otherworldliness. There were people who seemed to think of nothing else but the great last drama at the close of the age, when the Son of Man would come in the clouds of glory . . . For Jesus, the kingdom is much more immediate than that. When the RSV translates the Greek (*entos hymōn*) as 'in the midst of you', the translators are correcting a popular modern misconception, viz., that it means 'within you' as some kind of spiritual experience or endowment. If we were to adopt such a translation, the text might well seem contradictory in the extreme: the kingdom is not 'here' nor 'there' but 'here' (i.e., 'within')! If, however, we follow the RSV, we must ask what the phrase 'in the midst of you' means. This is where the notion of the creation of space is helpful. In his parable and ministry, Jesus is enacting and projecting new horizons of the kingdom. And new horizons broaden our existing world – the world in which we may be frustrated or suffocated, in which we may have lost worth or direction – by allowing us to move forward into a new area of meaning or activity in which we can begin to make fresh discoveries about ourselves, our fellows, our world and God. The kingdom is always 'in the midst of you' – it has to do with the world of people, the world of God's creation. But this notion also implies 'the space into which you can move' i.e., space within a human context in which you can flourish without oppressing your neighbour.

The notion of Christ's ministry as 'boundary crossing' is equally evocative and receives celebrated expression in the parable of the Good Samaritan. The parable focussed on racial, social, religious and political divisions, all of which were represented in the Jew-Samaritan conflict. It is relatively easy to devise similar word-parables with a modern reference, but doing is much more effective than merely talking. Practical projects, by their very nature, transcend and neutralize such divisions, for people are brought together to share a priority concern for community; and community is a central expression of the kingdom. If community is once given the leading edge, then real challenges emerge to the way people, groups and institutions actually perform. And the churches are not immune to the scrutiny.

Deep within humanity, with all its insecurity, is the instinct for survival or self-preservation; and this motif is present in group and institutional behaviour. The impetus is to hold on, to preserve what one has, whether it is a job, a group, an institution that has outlived its usefulness, or some illusory security such as status or possessions. Jesus said, 'Let go': particularly let go unproductive cares and illusory securities. He could say 'Let go', because he held out the new horizons of God's kingdom towards which one could move. He could even point parabolically to the 'birds of the air' and the 'lilies of the field'. But here is no sixties-style 'drop-out' movement, in which the rejection of material values was so often linked with parasitical purposelessness. Within the horizons of the kingdom, worldly need is recognized: 'your heavenly Father knows you need all these things' (Matt. 6.32). They are set, however, in a new perspective which combines true dependence (ultimately on God) with true human initiative and purpose (the parable of the talents – Matt. 25.14–30). To change life-perspectives in this way involves a deep re-orientation, a transforming change denoted, in New Testament language, by the term 'repentance' – and that stands at the very entry to the kingdom. It is no doubt part of what Jesus meant by taking up one's cross: 'Whoever will save his life will lose it; and whoever loses his life for my sake and the gospel's will save it' (Mark 8.35).

Losing an unproductive or misguided life in order to gain a creative, purposeful one may even be an attractive prospect, although it may not be a painless process of transition. It is a prospect which brings hope to many, and hope is worth striving for – like the pearl of great price. But it is a different matter when we are asked to let go a precious project, a creative life-style, a life of service. This may be the experience of some who have worked steadfastly for a particular project, have seen it struggle to achieve a partial fulfilment of its goals, and then have 'success' snatched away as it is frustrated or dies. It is enough to make one cry out like Job. Such situations, of course, are complex. On the one hand, even the most dedicated worker, being human, is affected by worldly ideas of 'success'. Success is something we need for the sake of our self-esteem. And this worldly notion so often invades our estimate of spiritual activity – so many converts per night, such-and-such a growth rate in our church community, x per cent increase in 'Christian liberality'. Such factors may be taken – understandably, if precariously – as 'signs of the kingdom'. But many 'servants of the kingdom' do not see such evidences, and without support and encouragement may well descend into self-doubt. Yet the 'ministry of the kingdom' meant, for Jesus, letting go the relatively 'successful' work in Galilee and setting his face steadfastly towards Jerusalem, knowing that what awaited him there was rejection and death (cf. Mark 8.31; 9.31; 10.33f.). The earthly ministry terminated on a cross which bore the ironic superscription, 'the King of the Jews' – a new and different kind of parable. How does one justify this colossal sacrifice of the most creative of lives? The only satisfying way is that adopted by the evangelists, who see it in the context of his 'rising again' (all the 'passion predictions' just referred to culminate in the resurrection); or the apostolic preachers, who proclaim his lordship: 'God has made him both Lord and Christ, this Jesus whom you crucified' (Acts 2.36). Unless we see the kingdom as something far greater than our work, our project or our success, then the results of all our endeavours may be mere struggle, mere failure or untimely demise. If our work bears any fruit, it does so in the life of others in ways of which we may not be fully aware. Paul knew that his living was in fact a dying: 'death works in me, but life in you . . .' (II Cor. 4.12). Here is the 'letting-go' which is required of Christ's servants. It makes sense only in so far as we accept that, for all the 'worldliness' of God's kingdom, it is not confined to the world which we know. This world is part of a greater cosmos which God rules. In the future lies God's harvest, complete and assured, and any harvest we may have the good fortune to see here is but the merest first fruits of what shall eventually be. We must let it go – into God's hands.

Some projects lay emphasis on *shalom*, 'human flourishing' and on healing. In the gospel narratives, as we have noted above, certain categories of disablement are singled out for particular treatment: the blind, the deaf, the dumb; others include the poor and the imprisoned. Healing stories can be misleading. Of course such healings took place: we have no reason to doubt the fact. But Jesus did not cure all who were sick in his country, any more than there can be a guaranteed remedy for every infirmity today. Healing stories are 'signs': parables, we might say, of the kingdom. The blind have no vision, but can receive the vision of the kingdom; all are blind who lack it. The deaf 'hear' again; those who do not hear and understand the message of the kingdom are deaf. The dumb speak: those in deep bondage are unable to articulate their problems or their sufferings, or to communicate with others and receive support; they are crushed and oppressed – Paulo Freire has much to say about them in his *Pedagogy of the Oppressed* – their life is a prison, and Jesus broke the bars and set them free. The poor are both like and unlike the others: like them in that poverty can be a crushing burden, and for all such, the shepherdless sheep, Jesus had the deepest compassion. But 'the poor' are also blessed, because they have the true naivety of faith unencumbered by the false security and the cares of wealth or power: their powerlessness gives access to the power of the Spirit. There is no sentimentality here: the poor are people – God's people: theirs is the kingdom! Hence, all projects of the kingdom today are about *shalom* and for people: 'the things that belong to their peace'. And those needing to sense the presence of God's kingdom today include many who are searching for 'vision' to see the next few steps ahead. Many who need to 'hear' a message of assurance. Many who need to learn to speak again and reach out to others. Many who need to step out of their own particular prison-house.

Which leads us back, not before time, to spirituality and to Brother Harold and Shepherd's Law. If our discussion has achieved anything, it has emphasized the fact that, in relation to Jesus and the kingdom of God, the path to holiness lies through the world. Yet Jesus' withdrawal to a quiet place is one of the most characteristic features of his ministry (cf. Mark 1.35). There is a pattern of engagement–withdrawal–re-engagement. There is a time to preach, teach and heal; there is a time for solitude, meditation and spiritual renewal. And the two are inter-related. This inter-relationship is perhaps the hub of the issue. It is not difficult to recognize 'a new darkness' today, 'a new breed of lost, restless, questing barbarians'; nor to see the contemplative community as a place of vision as well as 'sanctuary for the broken and wounded to find healing and peace'. Various thoughts may be prompted by such reflections. The need for mission (Jesus proclaimed the kingdom; is our message presented with sufficient clarity and directness?). The need to make contact with outsiders, open up dialogue with them and be glad to be with them (cf. Jesus' table-fellowship with outsiders). The need to deepen the understanding, insight and faith of the churches (cf. Jesus' frequent sessions with the disciples alone). Or the need to preserve the light of Christian learning and devotion amid the gathering gloom (cf. the monasteries in the 'dark ages').

Some may wonder if the modern 'parables of action' presented above really go far enough. They suggest the gentleness of doves without perhaps the guile of the serpent, and in consequence people may take from them precisely what they want and nothing more. The great reservoir of spiritual meaning and purpose is untapped and neglected, a projection of the wishful thinking of its authors. Yet one impressive feature of the presentations is the authors' awareness and readiness to admit that this may indeed be so. Nor did Jesus himself avoid it: 'Truly, truly I say to you', the Jesus of the Fourth Gospel says to the crowds, 'you seek me, not because you saw signs, but because you ate your fill of the loaves' (John 6.26). Mixed motivation is part of human living, and we should not be oppressed at the thought of 'being used'. There is always the need to provide the cup of cold water in Jesus' name; wherever that is done, a parable is enacted. And this may well be a 'beginning of parables'; the first step on a way which may, under God, be the turning-point in a life that will be 'opened' to the Spirit. Nevertheless, the 'culture gap' between church and outsider, so uncharacteristic of Jesus himself, must occasion great alarm in the churches. For to them has been given the supreme parable of the kingdom.

On the eve of his death, Jesus celebrated the last supper with his disciples: a 'memorable' occasion, on which he said, 'Truly, I say to you, I shall not drink again of the fruit of the vine until that day when I drink it new in the kingdom of God' (Mark 14.25). In this act, therefore, something richly evocative of the kingdom is performed: some telling anticipation of the kingdom is given. And what is the act but the breaking, the sharing, the giving of himself to his followers and through them to the world? A sharing in the context of thanksgiving and celebration, of fellowship and unity and the renewal of the covenant with God. It is here that all parables of the kingdom come into one single focus. Here is the deepest insight into the mystery of the kingdom uniting meditation and action, the material and the spiritual, this world and the next. If, in our fragmented world, many who are in need are as yet far off from the table, then it may be our calling to take to them 'in our own bodies' something of the reality of the self-giving Christ. Thus will 'all our endeavours, begun, continued and ended in him' be sacraments – signs, parables – of the kingdom.

Opposite, clockwise from top:
Minsteracres Community Resource Centre, Brunswick Methodist Church with Listening Post, Kirknewton School Campaign, Waddington Street Day Centre, Traidcraft Shop sign.